EYEWITNESS TO EARLY
REFORM IN MYANMAR

EYEWITNESS TO EARLY REFORM IN MYANMAR

TREVOR WILSON

Australian
National
University

PRESS

ASIAN STUDIES SERIES MONOGRAPH 7

ANU PRESS

Published by ANU Press
The Australian National University
Acton ACT 2601, Australia
Email: anupress@anu.edu.au
This title is also available online at press.anu.edu.au

National Library of Australia Cataloguing-in-Publication entry

Creator:	Wilson, Trevor, author.
Title:	Eyewitness to early reform in Myanmar / Trevor Wilson.
ISBN:	9781925022988 (paperback) 9781925022995 (ebook)
Series:	Asian studies series monograph.
Subjects:	Democratization--Burma.
	Government, Resistance to--Burma.
	Burma--Politics and government--1988-
Dewey Number:	320.9591

Cover design and layout by ANU Press. Cover photograph: *Golden Rock Kyaiktiyo at Dawn* by David Wansbrough.

Contents

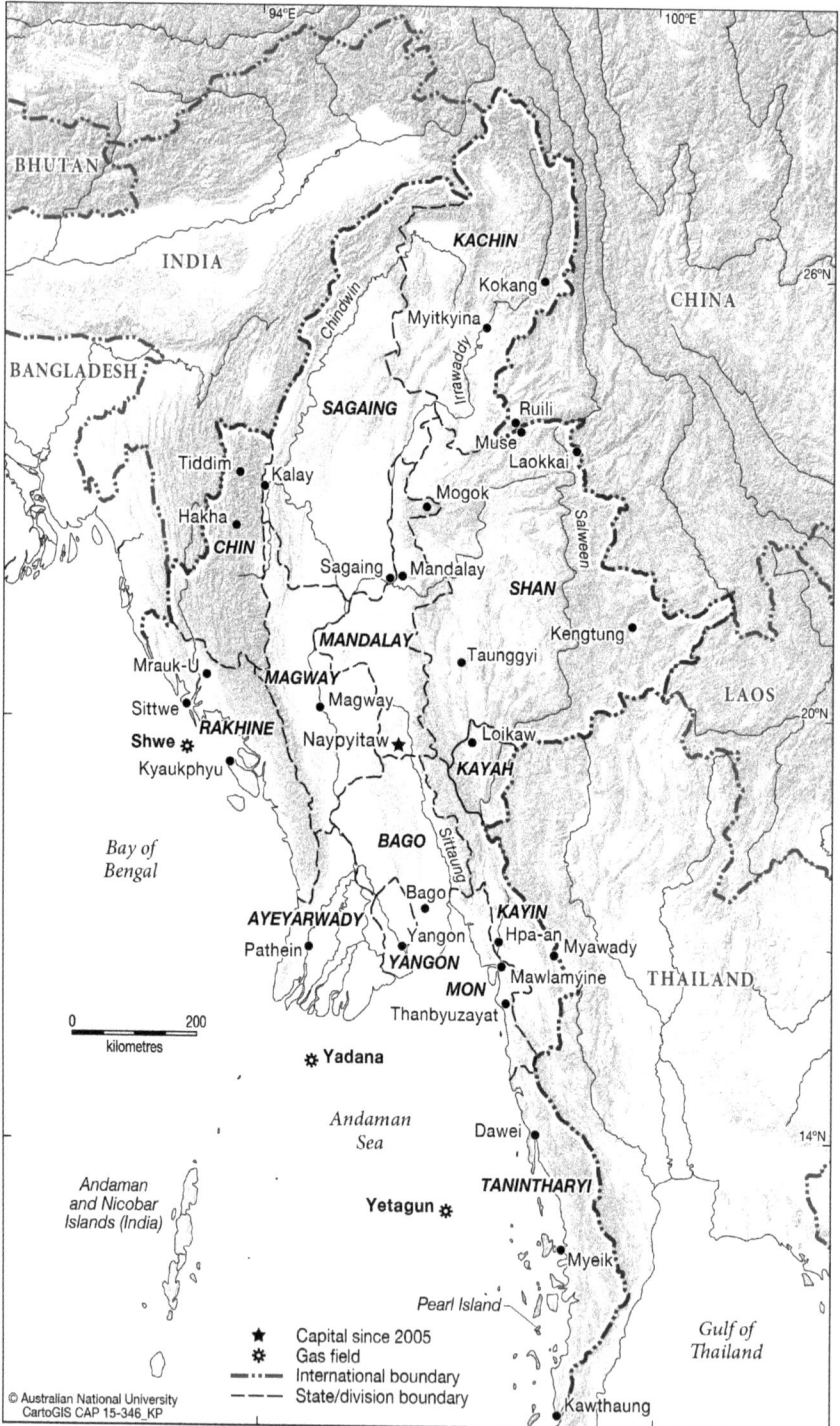

Map of Myanmar/Burma

Source: The Australian National University CartoGIS

Preface

The period between 1999 and 2003 proved to be quite an interesting period in modern Myanmar history, because it provided unusual insights into the political and other forces that propelled Myanmar on its pathway towards a transition to democracy. My assignment as Australian Ambassador from 2000 to mid-2003 enabled me to obtain some unique perspectives on current developments in Myanmar, which I was able to refine and extend over the next 10 years or so, after my 'early' retirement from the Australian foreign service and while a Visiting Fellow on Myanmar at The Australian National University (2003–2015).

Why was this period especially interesting or illuminating? Why is it still worth recording in some form some time later? One obvious answer is that some of the specific origins of Myanmar's current transition trace their start and many of their enduring characteristics to this period, which made this an unusually good opportunity — in terms of openness, access to people and places, and availability of data — to document these early encounters with reform. The second answer is that for those participating directly in attempts to transform and improve Myanmar — Myanmar people and foreigners alike — this period was an experimental laboratory. Some initiatives tried at this time worked and were perpetuated; some did not work and were modified or dropped.

My experience is not unique: some of my Australian colleagues shared similar experiences; some of my foreign colleagues also shared similar experiences. But much of this background is not well known, has not been widely or accurately reported, and is already being forgotten.

I was fortunate in several ways, mostly not of my own making: Australian policy towards Myanmar at this time — under Foreign Minister Alexander Downer in the Coalition Government of John Howard — was somewhat innovative; and I met many Australians working in and with Myanmar, some of whom had been doing so intelligently and empathetically for many years. I was also able to travel widely inside Myanmar and met many Myanmar people deeply committed to making their country a much better place. Most of these people remain good friends to this day.

I dedicate this book to those Myanmar people.

Acknowledgements

I am deeply grateful to former Department of Foreign Affairs colleagues who encouraged me in this enterprise, Lyndall MacLean and Michelle Chan. I appreciate the helpful comments and advice from Canberra friends and colleagues, Nicholas Farrelly, Morten Pedersen, and Andrew Selth, each of whom is a world-class expert on Myanmar. I could not have succeeded without the patient and wise support of ANU Press Asian Studies Editorial Committee chair Craig Reynolds. And most of all I received enormous support at the time of my assignment in Myanmar, and in the finalisation of this manuscript, from my wife and partner, Christine.

List of Acronyms and Abbreviations

ABC	Australian Broadcasting Corporation
ACIAR	Australian Centre for International Agricultural Research
ACTU	Australian Council of Trade Unions
AFP	Australian Federal Police
ALP	Australian Labor Party
APEC	Asia-Pacific Economic Cooperation
APHEDA	Australian People for Health, Education and Development Abroad
ASEAN	Association of Southeast Asian Nations
ATVI	Australia Television International
AusAID	Australian Agency for International Development
BANCA	Biodiversity and Nature Conservation Association
BBC	British Broadcasting Corporation
CARE	Cooperative for Assistance and Relief Everywhere
CCDAC	Central Committee on Drug Abuse Control
CRP	Committee for a Representative Parliament
DAP	Direct Assistance Program
DFAT	Department of Foreign Affairs and Trade
ESCAP	Economic and Social Commission for Asia and the Pacific
EU	European Union
FREDA	Forest Resource Environment Development and Conservation Association
ICG	International Crisis Group

ICRC	International Committee of the Red Cross
ILO	International Labour Organization
INGO	International Non-Governmental Organisation
ITC	Information and Communications Technology
KIO	Kachin Independence Organisation
LDC	Least Developed Country
MANA	Myanmar Anti-Narcotics Association
MMA	Myanmar Medical Association
MOU	Memorandum of Understanding
MPF	Myanmar Police Force
MRC	Myanmar Red Cross
NCGUB	National Coalition Government of the Union of Burma
NLD	National League for Democracy
NMSP	New Mon State Party
NPO	Non-Profit Organisation
NSW	New South Wales
OECD	Organisation for Economic Co-operation and Development
ONA	Office of National Assessments
POW	Prisoner of War
OSS	Office of Strategic Studies
SBS	Special Broadcasting Service
SLORC	State Law and Order Restoration Council
SPDC	State Peace and Development Council
UN	United Nations
UNDCP	United Nations International Drug Control Programme
UNDP	United Nations Development Programme
UNICEF	United Nations Children's Fund
UNHCR	United Nations High Commissioner for Refugees
USDP	Union Solidarity and Development Party
VOA	Voice of America
WHO	World Health Organization
YMCA	Young Men's Christian Association

1

Introduction

In 2000, Myanmar/Burma was one of the least known countries in Southeast Asia, despite its history as a long-time British colony, and its place as a scene of significant and sustained international military action during World War II. Decades of self-imposed isolation by military-dominated governments, followed by over a decade of international sanctions, contributed not only to this lack of understanding and knowledge, but also to the prevalence of a variety of international stereotypes about the country and its people. It was seen as a 'backwater', as being of little economic or cultural significance, and its people were believed to be uncomfortable with foreigners.

Myanmar/Burma was best known as a country of military dictatorship and political repression, and attempts by the international community to develop effective policies to change this situation were often presented in mainstream analyses as being either misguided or without focus. Internationally, relatively few academics thoroughly studied the nature of politics, the military, or the state in Myanmar/Burma, and media reporting tended to be superficial and trivial.

This situation was not helped by the tendency for politics in Myanmar/Burma, and responses to political dilemmas, to be highly and unnecessarily polarised. The international community was always under enormous pressure to take sides in international debates over political issues in Myanmar; and, conversely, the government of Myanmar/Burma was expected to accept the majority international line on human rights, forced labour, economic development options, democratic institutions, and socio-economic choices. The situation was not helped by the lack of sustained, enquiring, and objective international journalism, given that the only foreign journalist based in Myanmar was from China's Xinhua News Agency.

Any visitor to Myanmar/Burma at the time soon discovered how wrong most of these stereotypes were. In fact, Myanmar/Burma is a country of substantial natural resources, with a long and rich cultural and artistic heritage. I found Myanmar people to be genuinely friendly and hospitable towards foreigners, with a proud and independent way of thinking, who complained little, and had developed many creative and innovative 'coping mechanisms'. Politically, Myanmar/Burma was a complex and complicated country facing physical, psychological, and financial obstacles in dealing with its many long-term problems, which the rest of the world seemed to prefer not to confront directly by providing assistance or relevant expertise. Many of the solutions that were offered by the international community — especially through the United Nations — were simplistic and tendered on a 'take it or leave it' basis.[1]

Probably only three Burmese individuals were well known in the rest of the world: U Nu, the non-aligned prime minister in the period after independence (various times between 1948–62); General Ne Win, the ruthless dictator whose xenophobic policies had virtually destroyed the country (1958–60, 1962–88); and Aung San Suu Kyi, whose winning of the Nobel Peace Prize in 1991 and whose subjection to years of house arrest by a ruthless military had transformed her into an

---

1   By 1999, relations between Myanmar and the World Bank had broken down over unauthorised disclosure of World Bank documentation about Myanmar; the US Congress had determined that no US Ambassador would be appointed to Myanmar/Burma; the West (as represented by the Organisation for Economic Co-operation and Development (OECD)) had severed practical cooperation with and training of the Burmese military, although the United States retained its defence attaché positions in Yangon; other international agencies (such as the International Labour Organization and the International Committee of the Red Cross) were experiencing difficulties establishing working relationships with Myanmar/Burma. But the UN Security Council — because of the veto powers of China and the Soviet Union/Russia — never imposed mandatory sanctions against Myanmar/Burma.

'icon' of democracy. Yet some Burmese diplomats and economists were famous in their fields, and some Burmese philosophers and historians produced original approaches to region-wide issues.[2]

Myanmar/Burma clearly presented the international community with a serious challenge, which was very hard to ignore given the prominence accorded Aung San Suu Kyi after she won the Nobel Peace Prize. Whenever the situation in Myanmar/Burma took a turn for the worse, whatever the cause, it seemed to highlight the inability of international pressure to force the military regime to change its approach and adopt a more conciliatory approach. (In fact, of course, it would have needed a bit more patience than either the international media or the US Congress could muster, both being impatient and one-sided in their attitudes.) Moreover, scholars at that time tended to transform any discussion into a debate about sanctions versus 'engagement', especially in the United States, where sanctions were always a favoured option of the US Congress or US administrations, even though the success of most sanctions regimes was highly questionable. Much of the academic argumentation about sanctions and engagement was also flawed — it was often highly ideological, sometimes plainly one-sided, and in general did not focus on benefits from engagement or damage from sanctions. The academic debate, like the policy 'debate', failed to take a strategic or multi-disciplined approach. Furthermore, everyone underestimated the determination of the Burmese military to hold onto power and to stay on their preferred course, which was later outlined in their 2004 'Seven-Point Road Map'.

While Australia was unmistakeably a supporter of sanctions, and therefore only partially and occasionally 'friendly' towards the regime through its policy of 'limited engagement', officials in the Myanmar/Burma Government and the ordinary Burmese people were unfailingly polite and civil about this difference of viewpoint. There was clearly a strong legacy of goodwill and trust towards Australia, even many years after the Colombo Plan finished. (However, many Burmese — who became friends — were open in interchanges I had with them about their opposition to sanctions, which they saw as only harming poor people and the country, and having little or no impact on the

---

2   Here one thinks of UN Secretary-General U Thant; development economist Professor Hla Myint; Aung San Suu Kyi herself on pacifism; and Dr Thant Myint-U on history.

military leadership.) Their opinions influenced me into thinking the same way, though as ambassador I always had to support Australian policy. This is why I wrote about the 'collateral damage' being caused by sanctions in 2007, long after I ceased being ambassador.

In hindsight, one can see that the period between 2000–03 was an experimental reform period. What was in play then were numerous ideas and changes that took their time to take root and to develop fully, but which included some measures that would eventually prove not only successful but also popular. Looking back, it is interesting to identify any indicators of how and why certain changes were effective, or at least non-threatening, and what reforms might be important for a successful political transition.

One issue that had long provoked debate, and which would remain a topic for debate for many years, was what name should be used for Myanmar/Burma. Obviously, the way the incoming State Law and Order Restoration Council (SLORC) changed the name to Myanmar in 1989 was a political action. While it might not have been their first action, it was clearly made in such a way as to indicate the defining nature of the change. On the other hand, it can hardly have been a surprising move, since the term 'Myanmar' had been in widespread official and day-to-day use for many years. The decision by the democracy movement to object to the change of name is equally a political action, and some of the reasons they cite for objecting to it do not seem very persuasive. Most people from Myanmar who take up the issue are arguing from a political perspective, whatever they say, so it is hard to pinpoint the objective case for or against 'Myanmar' or 'Burma'.

Interestingly, the debate over nomenclature was conducted mostly outside the country, not inside; it mattered more to the exiles and refugees from 'Burma' than to the residents of the country. The names became highly politicised after 1988, when the newly formed democracy movement used 'Burma' without exception: for example, the 'Free Burma Campaign', the National Coalition Government for the Union of Burma (NCGUB), and the 'Burma Campaigns' in the United States, the UK, and Australia.

Since my letters of credence as ambassador referred to the country as 'Myanmar', for reasons of protocol I always maintained that the name 'Myanmar' was correct, and then found it was by far the most commonly used name inside the country. Indeed, the only residents of the country who always used 'Burma' at this time were National League for Democracy (NLD) members and the elderly, who had been accustomed to saying 'Burma' for most of their lives. In Australia, I did not always insist on 'Myanmar' if my interlocutor was clearly more comfortable with 'Burma', but I did deliberately use 'Myanmar' when being interviewed by Voice of America, just as they deliberately used 'Burma' when questioning me.

Otherwise, I was relatively unconcerned about what the country should be called, and tended to avoid becoming embroiled in the ongoing debates about this, which I still regard as an issue of little consequence.[3] In a practical sense, most Western diplomats — including my successors and I — would have followed the custom that prevailed in the environment in which they were speaking (or writing). Australian governments of both persuasions have more than once changed their position on nomenclature, and then sometimes reversed that position, which did not increase clarity, certainty, or understanding on the part of the Australian public.[4] However, since so many people and organisations made an issue of the name used for the country, the Australian Embassy resorted to using two different letterheads, one using 'Yangon' and 'Myanmar', and another using 'Rangoon' and 'Burma'.

Australia did not follow the military regime, or the United Nations, when they switched to 'Myanmar' in 1989. In late 1995, then Foreign Minister Gareth Evans decided to move to use 'Myanmar', after Burma/Myanmar started being raised (as 'Myanmar') in Association of Southeast Asian Nations (ASEAN) meetings which Australia attended, but this policy did not last very long. When the conservative Coalition Government assumed power in March 1996, they supported the name

---

3   Andrew Selth probably provided the most balanced and objective account of this in his 27 November 2013 piece on the Lowy Interpreter blog: www.lowyinterpreter.org/post/2013/11/27/Australia-and-the-BurmaMyanmar-name.aspx?COLLCC=178848935&.
4   For an example of a media release Gareth Evans issued as foreign minister, see: foreignminister.gov.au/releases/1995/m115.html.

'Burma'.[5] (This did not stop the new minister Alexander Downer developing his own innovative approach to engaging with the military regime in Burma/Myanmar.) After 2007, as foreign minister and then prime minister, Kevin Rudd used 'Burma'. Thus Australian financial sanctions were legislated in 2007 using 'Burma'. (They were originally drafted under Alexander Downer and then taken up by Kevin Rudd.) However, when Bob Carr became foreign minister in the Gillard Labor Government and visited the country in mid-2012, he initiated a complete shift to 'Myanmar', which the Australia media and others eventually followed. Official Australian usage remained 'Myanmar' until late 2013, when Foreign Minister Julie Bishop quietly ordered a complete change, and all entries on the Department of Foreign Affairs and Trade (DFAT) website were changed.[6] (For a time, examples of both terms could be found on the DFAT website, with historical references to 'Myanmar' on the former Australian Agency for International Development (AusAID) website being among the last to be removed.) By this time, most of the world media were using 'Myanmar', and the country was in the public eye as the host of ASEAN and East Asian Summit meetings as 'Myanmar'. (Australian Government ministers attended most of these meetings.)

The Australian media were among the last in the world to change to using 'Myanmar'; even the *New York Times* and the *Wall Street Journal* had adjusted their terminology in 2012, after the by-elections for the Myanmar Parliament, in which the National League for Democracy participated, thereby acknowledging the correctness of the usage by the military regime and its successor, the Thein Sein Government. I and other 'experts' on the country, who were often interviewed by the Australian Broadcasting Corporation (ABC) and Special Broadcasting Service (SBS), had long urged the Australian media to adopt an apolitical approach and to follow the United Nations practice, but such arguments were to no avail. Both the ABC and the SBS seemed to be in the thrall of Aung San Suu Kyi and the NLD, and instinctively and stubbornly followed democracy movement wishes.

---

5   See Alexander Downer's firm response to repression of NLD activities by the military regime as the new foreign minister: foreignminister.gov.au/releases/1996/fa102.html.
6   No public explanation of this change was issued, but, when asked, DFAT explained the policy along the lines of: 'The [Australian] Government will use the term "Myanmar" in communications with and public statements about the Myanmar Government, but "Burma" in other contexts.' Private communication from DFAT.

When the new President of Myanmar, Thein Sein, visited Australia officially in early March 2013 and the Australian Government for protocol reasons had to use 'Myanmar', it was obviously awkward for the media to ignore this. When the ABC finally changed its practice in early 2013, they could not resist having a special radio item on the subject (for which they conspicuously did not interview me).[7]

Some of the arguments used in the name debate to make the case for 'Burma' are blatantly wrong and misleading. For example, it is not correct that 'Burma' was chosen through a democratic process in 1947 in contrast to the way the military regime changed the name in 1989; nor is it true that the name 'Burma' is more acceptable to the ethnic minorities in Myanmar; if anything, 'Myanmar' is more acceptable to ethnic groups because it carries no racial or ethnic overtones, in contrast to 'Burma', which plainly derives from the majority ethnic name 'Bamar'.

Common international usage is not necessarily much of a guide to what is 'best' or 'correct' practice in using such terminology. Governments were always influenced by political factors, producing the undesirable result of Asia and the Third World using 'Myanmar' and the West using 'Burma'. Foreign travel companies, not surprisingly, opted for the least risky option of sticking with 'Burma'. Scholars started to choose, citing a variety of reasons — some adopted a historical approach, using 'Myanmar' from 1989. Many writers used 'Burma' without disclosing a political reason for doing so, occasionally without understanding the political significance of what they were doing. Fortunately, the internet can easily be programmed to accept both Burma and Myanmar equally and as equivalents.

Making the name of the country a high-profile policy issue and provoking debate that is not always well-informed is at least a distraction and at worst not helpful in terms of substantive relationship and activities. A former British Ambassador to Thailand, Derek Tonkin, who has become a 'realist' activist on Myanmar, has been quite scathing about the negative effects of recent reversion to the terminology 'Burma' by a few:

---

7   See Liam Cochrane's 22 March 2013 story on Radio Australia: www.radioaustralia.net.au/international/radio/program/connect-asia/is-it-burma-or-myanmar/1105814.

The policies of those Western countries which maintain this unedifying dichotomy reflect a veritable schizophrenia in dealing with what is very much a self-imposed dilemma. 'Myanmar' is all too often an operational necessity — not a mere diplomatic courtesy as the US State Department would have us believe — where all matters of diplomacy, trade and international relations are concerned, while 'Burma' is still used in a domestic context, to pander to the activist lobby and to respond to the entreaties of Daw Aung San Suu Kyi. The reality is that 'Myanmar' is essential on all matters that count, since governmental and commercial business would otherwise grind to a halt. But 'Burma' can be used when there is supposedly nothing at stake. What a quaint way to conduct inter-state relations!

The recent [2013] change in Australian policy, if confirmed, will neither advance reconciliation between Suu Kyi and the Generals, nor help Australian national interests. It is a classic example of the folly of politicians succumbing to short-term interest on a wave of emotion when a cool head, reliability as a prospective partner and support for the reform process in Myanmar should be primary considerations. How counterproductive can you get![8]

---

8   See Derek Tonkin's Network Myanmar website: www.networkmyanmar.org/.

2

The Historical Contexts

Conditions in Myanmar in 2000

Being assigned to Myanmar/Burma obviously meant being prepared to function as a diplomatic representative in a political, social, and economic context created by Burma's own history and its own actions or 'decisions'. One needed to be aware of the country's British colonial past as well as more recent events, not the least of which was the 1988 pro-democracy uprising, and the infamous and repressive military regime that followed, whose continued existence still dominated almost every aspect of life in the country for its own citizens and those foreigners living and working there. I quickly discovered that although Burma was a relatively small country with very modest impact on the outside world, for a variety of reasons it generated a wealth of scholarly and media attention, perhaps even to a disproportionate extent. There was not only a good deal of historical and other writing about Burma, which was of great assistance in carrying out my assignment, but there was also more media attention than one would expect for a relatively isolated country. Media attention could be a mixed blessing, requiring a great deal of care and alertness at all times, since as ambassador it would not always be possible to avoid it altogether.[1]

---

1   In the early 2000s, the Department of Foreign Affairs and Trade (DFAT) was not as restrictive as it was to later become in regard to media contacts, allowing our ambassadors a small amount of leeway for factual comment to journalists. I found that, because there was not a large number of 'Western' embassies in Yangon, and because reliable sources of public information were scarce, I would often be sought out by journalists from other countries as well as from Australia. Indeed, Australia's ambassador seemed to be relied on by quite a number of foreign journalists to provide helpful and balanced observations.

One ongoing challenge, however, was the fact that much of the outside media and academic interest in Myanmar was to a greater or lesser extent influenced by political and/or ideological considerations. In other words, it was sometimes biased and not objective, responding to or reflecting a predetermined 'agenda'. For example, reporting in some organisations funded by pro-democracy institutions (such as the US government–backed National Endowment for Democracy or the private Soros Open Society Foundation) in outlets such as *The Irrawaddy* or *BurmaNet News* is always enormously valuable and fills very real gaps, but in its coverage, content, and choice of topics, it is never politically neutral. Outsiders did not always immediately understand this.

Two aspects of Myanmar's turbulent history probably stood out for their far-reaching consequences and impacts: one is the extent of its isolation, first self-imposed during decades of authoritarian rule, and lately reinforced by various political and economic sanctions imposed by 'Western' — or, more correctly, Organisation for Economic Co-operation and Development (OECD) — countries; the other was the continued existence of martial law in the form of a military regime that had assumed power as a supposed temporary measure to restore 'law and order' in 1988, and then sabotaged the reconciliation process it had set up to transfer power to an elected government. While the 'disturbances' of 1988 are often characterised as a 'democratic uprising' against the (authoritarian but elected) government of the day, this is only part of the story.[2] Starting on 8 August, students and workers launched protests and demonstrations in Yangon that spread quickly to many other cities across the country. A general strike soon followed, and business conditions deteriorated. Between 8 August and 18 September 1988, there was a collapse of law and order, with indiscriminate mob violence targeted at the authorities, especially police, and public executions by civilians on the streets. The army's crackdown led to an estimated 3,000 people being killed over the period of the uprising, in incidents that are still seared in the minds of participants and observers, from young students to townspeople.

---

2   Several accounts exist of the events of 1988–90. One of the most accessible is *Outrage* by the well-known journalist Bertil Lintner, then working for the *Far Eastern Economic Review*. The most authoritative insider account is that by Dr Maung Maung, who as Attorney General was the only civilian in the Ne Win Government: U Maung Maung, *The 1988 Uprising in Burma*. New Haven, Connecticut: Yale University Southeast Asia Studies, 1999.

The 1990 election campaign itself was relatively peaceful, and resulted in the newly formed National League for Democracy (NLD) winning a majority of seats, with a voter turn-out of 72 per cent. However, the elections occurred without the participation of Aung San Suu Kyi, who had emerged as a leader of the protest movement in August 1988, but had been placed under house arrest by the military. When the military regime — the State Law and Order Restoration Council (SLORC) — proposed convening a National Convention to draft a new constitution rather than transferring power, there was understandably widespread disappointment, and a large number of activists left the country when warrants for their arrest were issued. Soon afterwards, in December 1990, a coalition government-in-exile was set up — the National Coalition Government of the Union of Burma (NCGUB) — led by Aung San Suu Kyi's cousin, Dr Sein Win, who was one of the NLD MPs elected in 1990. The NCGUB was based in Washington DC, and it engaged in continuous lobbying on behalf of the democracy movement in Washington and New York. But it always had problems communicating effectively with the NLD inside the country, essentially because of relentless restrictions on political activity under the military regime. The NCGUB deferred to Suu Kyi, but was not always well informed about Suu Kyi's thinking. Suu Kyi, for her part, sought to avoid opening gaps between herself and the NCGUB, but regarded herself and the NLD's Central Executive Committee as the decision makers. The NCGUB was never a serious alternative government; its political profile was effectively lowered after the Committee for a Representative Parliament (CRP) was established in 1998 by those 1990 MPs remaining inside the country. The NCGUB was formally abolished in 2011 after the new parliament, made up of MPs elected in 2010, was convened.

When the SLORC announced in 1990 that it would not transfer power to the party that won the election, the international community reacted strongly to the human rights abuses of 1988 as well as this refusal to recognise election results, even though the world was preoccupied with the collapse of Eastern Europe and Gorbachev's reforms in the Soviet Union. The initial reaction of the international community took the form of political sanctions organised by international assistance donors through the OECD: government-to-government relations were restricted, economic assistance (but not humanitarian assistance) was stopped, most defence relations were suspended, and many governments issued statements criticising the SLORC. Developments in Burma were also raised in the United Nations: at the first opportunity, a group of mainly Western countries prepared a resolution for the 1991 UN General Assembly; in 1992, the UN Secretary-General appointed a special rapporteur (Professor Yozo Yokota of Japan); and later the United Nations Commission on Human Rights appointed a series of special rapporteurs on human rights. It was not possible politically to take the situation in Burma to the UN Security Council for the imposition of universal mandatory sanctions, because of the likelihood of a veto being exercised by China and the Soviet Union. The main thrust of the international response was to isolate and punish the Burmese military regime, with any form of engagement or consultation becoming a low priority. This stand-off would eventually provide the spark for a long-lasting debate about the merits of sanctions versus engagement.

These developments created a situation where the highly polarised domestic political situation in Myanmar was paralleled by a high degree of polarisation within the international community. Highly confrontational behaviour inside Myanmar was matched by hard-line ideological positions among Western members of the international community, the outcome of which was essentially a stalemate, with no substantive progress. Other key 'stakeholders' — such as China, India, or Association of Southeast Asian Nations (ASEAN) countries — were virtually marginalised in the political and diplomatic negotiations that ensued, and neutral or 'third party' mediation was effectively ruled out. Inside Myanmar, other political parties and ethnic groups struggled to advance their particular interests under military rule, and by 2000 they too had failed to achieve any real impact. International opinion was seriously divided, with Myanmar's Asian neighbours and Third World countries not prepared to endorse sanctions against Myanmar, preferring instead various forms of engagement with the military regime, which equally produced little evidence of progress. After more than a decade, it looked as if this prolonged stalemate in Myanmar could continue indefinitely.[3] Given the circumstances,

---

3   The best account of the protracted tensions between engagement and isolation in relation to Myanmar is Morten B. Pedersen's *Promoting Human Rights in Burma: A Critique of Western Sanctions Policies,* Lanham, Maryland: Rowman & Littlefield, 2008.

it is not surprising that many observers were disposed to give up on Myanmar. Nor was there any obvious potential solution available that had not already been tried.

From around the mid-1990s, and especially after 1999, the military regime began to experiment quietly and gradually with its own 'reform' program. Initially, from 1995, the regime started to open its borders to humanitarian international non-governmental organisations (INGOs) such as Word Vision, Médecins Sans Frontières, and the Cooperative for Assistance and Relief Everywhere (CARE), who were permitted to carry out humanitarian activities in different parts of the country. In 1997, Myanmar became a member of ASEAN and agreed to conform with ASEAN policies and procedures. In the same year, the regime self-nominated as a Least Developed Country (LDC) in the United Nations, and began accepting assistance from UN agencies. Between 1995 and October 2000, Aung San Suu Kyi was under restricted movement around Yangon and, while she could not carry out normal political activities, she would give speeches to her supporters across the wall of her residence. She continued to be harassed, was denied access to the media, foreign visitors, and members of her party, the National League for Democracy, and was often under house arrest.[4] Nevertheless, in 1999 the regime had issued an order outlawing forced labour, although they did not implement this until after they signed a cooperation MOU (Memorandum of Understanding) with the International Labour Organization (ILO) in 2002. In 1999 they agreed to an Australian proposal for human rights training preparatory to setting up an independent National Human Rights Commission (which they did not do until 2011). In the second half of the 1990s, relations with United Nations envoys and the World Bank were troubled, and the military regime was unresponsive to requests for visits.[5] However, from 2000, they agreed to regular visits by UN special envoys and special rapporteurs on human rights, and from 2002 allowed the ILO to open an office in Yangon. From May 2002, Aung San Suu Kyi was released from house arrest and permitted to travel freely around the country for the first time since 1989, and she and her party were

---

4   Aung Zaw, Founder and Editor-in-Chief of The Irrawaddy magazine has published on-line a reasonably accurate summary of Khin Nyunt's role in his *The Dictators: Part 8—Khin Nyunt Overplays his Hand*, available at: www.irrawaddy.com/feature/the-dictators-part-8-khin-nyunt-overplays-his-hand.html.
5   See Anna Magnusson and Morten Pedersen, *A Good Office?: Twenty Years of UN Mediation in Myanmar*, New York: International Peace Institute, 2012.

allowed to carry out limited political activities (and open party offices) around the country. All of this came to a brutal end in May 2003, when the regime instigated an attack on Aung San Suu Kyi while she was travelling around Myanmar, and she was again placed under house arrest.

Why abandoning the quest for an internationally assisted solution in Myanmar was not really an option is not hard to see. First, serious human rights abuses represented ongoing problems that could not be ignored, especially when prominent political prisoners such as Aung San Suu Kyi were part of the equation. Second, the socio-economic conditions for the people of Myanmar were manifestly disastrous and could not be allowed to drag on because of the enormous human costs. Third, the destabilising regional and strategic forces could not continue to be downplayed or denied — whether it was the spill-over into regional neighbours of transnational crime effects (refugees, people trafficking, narcotics trafficking) or the unhealthy and distorting strategic and military competition between China and India over Myanmar. So whether the outcomes of any initiatives in relation to Myanmar would be worthwhile or sufficient to justify the further efforts, and whether they might need to be contested or warrant subsequent confirmation would probably remain to be seen. At the same time, given the amount of misunderstanding or ignorance of other parties that was objectively prevalent regarding the situation in Myanmar/Burma, missteps and miscalculations might have contributed to the lack of progress. So it might always be worth another try, a slightly different approach, or better coordinated arrangements.

However, the level of mistrust and suspicion from the population towards the authorities (military and non-military) was massively deepened in later years by the ineptitude of the government's handling of fuel price increases in 2007 and its response to Cyclone Nargis in 2008, which inevitably spilled over into attitudes between the two opposing political groups. Most of the military and civilian figures responsible in the government at the time of the 1988 uprising had long since moved aside, leaving successor generations to manage the consequences. Economic and social damage to the country was long-lasting and severe. Unsurprisingly, this extreme political confrontation and polarisation was very apparent even more than a decade later, when I took up my position as ambassador, and has still not been fully overcome.

The state of Australia–Myanmar relations in 2000

Australian ambassadors represent the Australian Government in the countries to which they are appointed or accredited. They are formally in charge of all embassy staff, whether they are from DFAT or other departments, and whether they are posted to the country from Australia — 'Australia-based staff' — or whether they are recruited in the country — either nationals of the country, or third-country nationals: 'locally engaged staff'. Managing the embassy, which involves both overseeing its administration as well as providing leadership for the whole embassy, is the single most important role and responsibility of an ambassador. In the Australian foreign service, for many decades the ambassador's role and responsibilities have been spelled out formally in a letter of appointment (the 'Head of Mission Directive'), which also represents the statement of expectations against which an ambassador's performance is to be measured. But, of course, ambassadors are inevitably representatives of their country as well, not just the government. There are, however, no structured ways for this wider representative role to be monitored or assessed. An ambassador is meant to be an advocate for his own country, and an interpreter of the country to which he is assigned.

Operationally, ambassadors are regularly sent instructions to convey messages from the Australian Government to the government to which they are accredited. But they are also expected to use their own initiative to routinely convey generic messages or relevant policy statements to the government to which they are accredited, without specific instructions. To be an effective and objective interpreter of the country to which they are accredited, ambassadors are expected to develop a wide range of well-informed and influential contacts inside and outside the government to which they are accredited, and to send assessments and reports to Canberra from time to time to assist the process of formulating well-focused Australian policy towards the country to which they are accredited. Obviously, all of this requires frequent and effective communications — formal and informal — with relevant staff in the Australian Government. One of the underlying objectives in all of this is to avoid either government being 'surprised' by developments; but another important — absolutely normal and well understood — objective is to influence the policies of the government to which ambassadors are accredited. Surrounding this role is, of course, the routine requirement to engage in appropriate public relations activities of all kinds, both in Australia (although only occasionally) and in the country to which an ambassador is accredited (pretty well all of the time). It goes without saying that ambassadors are expected to be impartial and of the highest personal integrity. Nowadays, ambassadors are required to attend special 'head of mission' training programs in Canberra before they take up their assignments.

In Australia, foreign policy is not the exclusive preserve of DFAT, but is the product of a collective political process, which assumes considerable public acceptance of the central direction and the main content of the policy.[6] Ambassadors are expected to be conversant with all aspects of policy and mindful of opportunities or risks for Australia wherever they might arise. They might hope to influence the various elements of policy towards another country, region, or organisation, but are not expected to 'play favourites' by giving preference to one aspect of relations over others.

While it was not the accepted view at the time, it is clear now that by the end of the twentieth century Australia's relations with Burma/Myanmar had more to look backward on than to look forward to. It could reasonably be seen as a situation where all concerned were under-achieving and accepting missed opportunities, as was inevitable in the circumstances. There is no one in particular to blame for this; it arose primarily out of conditions in Burma that were not promising in terms of normal international relations.

One important exception to this general lack of interest in Myanmar was the fact that Foreign Minister Alexander Downer, in the Liberal–National Party Coalition Government of Prime Minister John Howard (1996–2007), showed considerable interest in Burma, and met his Myanmar counterparts (Ohn Gyaw and later Win Aung) reasonably regularly at ASEAN-Plus ministerial meetings between 1996 and 2007. While not changing Australia's political sanctions against

---

6   The most authoritative account of how Australian foreign policy is practised is still Allan Gyngell and Michael Wesley *Making Australian Foreign Policy*, Cambridge: Cambridge University Press, 2003.

Myanmar, in 1999 Downer showed considerable political courage and an innovative approach by launching Australian engagement initiatives with Myanmar in the field of human rights, police-to-police training, and — in 2002 — agricultural research collaboration. These were conducted by Monash University, the Australian Federal Police, and the Australian Centre for International Agricultural Research (ACIAR) respectively. These initiatives — each successful in its own way — added interest to my otherwise low-profile assignment. Downer himself made a short ministerial visit to Yangon in October 2002 during my period as Australian Ambassador, but unusually did not wish to receive a debriefing from me as outgoing ambassador at the end of my assignment in June 2003.

Trade between Australia and Myanmar, officially 'neither encouraged nor discouraged' since 1988, was minuscule by 2000, Australian exports averaging a mere $17 million per year between 1998 and 2003.[7] Consistent with this, Austrade withdrew its trade commissioner from the Australian Embassy following the imposition of commercial sanctions from 1988, after which trade commissioners would occasionally visit from the Australian Embassy in Bangkok, but really could do little more than maintain a 'watching brief'. Austrade never really reconsidered their position, and when their only long-serving Myanmar trade assistant died in 2002, they were (unsurprisingly) not especially concerned about having nobody to cover Myanmar. Larger Australian companies such as BHP had closed their Yangon offices, and one private Burmese trade consultant was able to represent the Australian Wheat Board, mining companies, and still take on other Australian clients. A small number of small-scale Australian companies were operating in fields such as environmental engineering, water treatment, and were making their mark in a tiny market. Mining support services for the large-scale copper mine then operated by Ivanhoe Minerals near Monywa in central Myanmar were coming from Western Australia on an entirely commercial basis.

---

7   Australian Bureau of Statistics figures. This figure was probably inaccurate, however, as it apparently did not include Australian goods shipped through Singapore but destined for Myanmar, where, by the early 2000s, newly opened supermarkets sold items such as King Island cheeses and Australian wines. There was no way to determine the size of entrepôt trade through Singapore.

The other significant Australian investment was in the *Myanmar Times* newspaper (see Chapter 8). Such people made up what was only a small community of individual Australian business people, but they were perhaps a sign of what might happen in the future.[8] The data on Australian trade with Myanmar is summarised in Table 1.

Table 1: Australian exports to Myanmar/Burma, 1991–2011

Year	Value ($AUD)	Including Wheat Exports (Australian Wheat Export Board data — no value given)
1991[1]	$3m	
1995[1]	$9m	
1999[2]	$14m	
2000[2]	$22m	56,331 tonnes
2001[2]	$38m	116,535 tonnes
2002[2]	$14m	73,140 tonnes
2003[2]	$10m	60,850 tonnes
2004[2]	$28m	69,600 tonnes
2005[2]	$38m	157,150 tonnes
2006[2]	$34m	139,500 tonnes
2007[2]	$34m	n/a
2008[2]	$33m	34,258 tonnes
2009[3]	$60m	n/a
2010[3]	$80m	n/a
2011[3]	$70m	n/a

Sources: (1) *The New ASEANS*, East Asia Analytical Unit, DFAT, 1997; (2) Australian Bureau of Statistics, Column 5368.0; (3) *Australia's Trade with East Asia* 2011, DFAT, August, 2012. Available at: www.dfat.gov.au/publications/stats-pubs/Australia-trade-with-east-asia-2011.pdf.

Australian trade was not only small, but was also dependant on a single commodity: wheat. Myanmar was a regular buyer of Australian wheat.

---

8   Austrade would not reopen an office in Yangon until early 2013, after the Australian Labor Party (ALP) Government lifted all economic sanctions against Myanmar.

Australia's aid program: Present and past

By 2000, Australian aid was also running at a very low level, restricted as it was to humanitarian and relief assistance, and with no funding of scholarships for training in Australia. By 2003–04, Australia's total aid flow would be only $7.8 million. This was not only a historical low level, but it did not by any measure reflect the needs of a least developed country with the lowest socio-economic data in ASEAN — lower even than Cambodia and Laos, countries with tiny populations compared to Myanmar's 50 million.

Australian aid to Myanmar by the year 2000 was not only minuscule, and deliberately styled 'humanitarian assistance', but it was also directed mainly through UN agencies, such as the World Food Programme and the United Nations Children's Fund (UNICEF), to avoid any suggestion that it was being channelled through the illegitimate military regime. After the military crackdown against the 1988 uprising, all Australian aid — with the exception of humanitarian assistance — to Myanmar had been halted as part of a concerted approach by Burma's traditional aid donors, namely the OECD countries, including Japan and later Korea. AusAID annual reports of this period ritualistically began their section on Burma by pronouncing that Australian aid to Burma was suspended after 1988. Even in 2001–02, when AusAID acknowledged that Burma was 'on the brink of a humanitarian crisis',[9] Australia's bilateral 'country program' for assistance to Myanmar was a mere $1.6 million. Throughout my term as ambassador, there was no appetite in Canberra for any expansion of the aid program (apart from the 'courageous' initiatives of Alexander Downer) and even my representations (along the lines of similar representations by my predecessors) for a resumption of Australian Government scholarships for individuals from Myanmar went without response. Yet, astonishingly, Australia was the only aid donor that completely stopped official scholarships: the United States continued its Fulbright scholarships, and Japan, the UK, and Germany continued their scholarship programs.

The data on Australian aid is summarised in Table 2.

---

9   AusAID Annual Report for 2001–02.

Table 2: Australian aid to Myanmar, 1999–2010

Year	Amount (Bilateral/Regional)	Percentage of total Australian official development assistance to East Asia	Total
1999–2000	A$0.8/NA	Not reported	Not reported
2000–01	A$1.4m/NA	Not reported	A$1.4m[1]
2001–02	A$1.6m/NA	Not reported	A$1.6m[2]
2002–03	A$3.0m/A$3.2m	Not reported	A$6.2m[3]
2003–04	A$2.9m	Less than 2%	A$8.7m[4]
2004–05	A$3.1m	Not reported	A$11.3m[5]
2005–06	A$3.4m	Less than 2%	A$12.2m[6]
2006–07	A$ 2.6m	2%	A$11.3m
2007–08	A$7.1m	2%	A$17.9m[7]
2008–09	A$6.9m	4%	A$44.9m[8]
2009–10	A$20.7m	3%	A$29.2m[9]

Sources: AusAID annual reports.

Notes: Since AusAID reports do not always disaggregate country program data and specific funding under cross-cutting programs, it can be hard to identify specific funding.

1. Funding for education support for 1,000 Burmese on the Thai–Burma border may not be included.
2. Funding for returning Rohingya refugees in Rakhine State may not be included.
3. Includes an amount for a bilateral child nutrition pilot program as well as funding for returning Rohingya refugees in Rakhine State.
4. Includes an amount for the 2003–06 Asian Regional Project Against People Trafficking, as well as funding for avian influenza prevention programs.
5. Includes funding for regional HIV/AIDS prevention program for intravenous drug users.
6. Includes funding for regional foot and mouth disease eradication programs as well as additional support for food and shelter for 160,000 Burmese living in camps on the Thai–Burma border.
7. Includes funding for humanitarian relief following Cyclone Nargis in May 2008. Also includes funding for livelihood support in Rakhine and Shan states.
8. Australia aid for Cyclone Nargis relief and recovery totalled A$55 million in 2008.
9. A new commitment to capacity building assistance in health, education, and agriculture announced by Foreign Minister Stephen Smith in February 2010.

It is sometimes not realised that in the post-war years, and after independence in 1948, Myanmar was more dependent on Colombo Plan technical assistance from Australia than from other donors. Myanmar came after Indonesia, India, Malaya, and Pakistan in the number of awards received for study in Australia, and was ahead of Sri

Lanka and other Southeast Asian countries. Burma was the fifth (out of 16) largest recipient of Australian Colombo Plan funds in the first eight years of the program.[10]

So it was not really surprising that, even in 2000, many Burmese still remembered Australia for the Colombo Plan — under which relatives might have been trained in Australia — whose passage into history was widely mourned, although not understood. Many Burmese openly wished for the return of those days. Even ministers and senior officers in the government would ask if Australia would resume aid along the lines of the Colombo Plan. For them, this was the single most perplexing anomaly in Australia's post-1988 policies. Scattered around the Myanmar civil service were senior technocrats who still traced their skills back to their education in Australia under the Colombo Plan. Thus the mining engineer who devised Myanmar's off-shore gas policy had a master's degree from Monash University, and a prominent Australian-trained doctor became Deputy Minister for Health in 2005 (he was the only Deputy Minister standing for the government Union Solidarity and Development Party (USDP) slate in the 2010 elections who was defeated).

Evidence of Australia's past extensive aid program surfaced from time to time even in the early 2000s, sometimes in unexpected situations. The north–south gravel road west of the Irrawaddy River, from Pathein to Monywa, which was built by the Snowy Mountains Engineering Corporation, was still referred to as 'the Australian road' or the 'Western Highway'; it was used mainly for transport of goods to markets, and was still in relatively good condition in 2000, although it was still unsealed. U Than Aye, the Minister for Education in the State Peace and Development Council (SPDC) Government for many years, was formerly the manager of the Australian Dairy Corporation's notorious Mandalay Dairy Project. When I visited water and sanitation projects on a UNICEF up-country trip in Sagaing Division in 2002, we saw a solar-powered village water supply system donated by Australia around 1988 — which was ahead of its time in operational

---

10   David Lowe and Daniel Oakman (eds), *Australia and the Colombo Plan 1949–1957*, Canberra: Australian Government Department of Foreign Affairs and Trade, 2004; 'The Colombo Plan's First Six Years: Australia's Part', (Doc. No. 299, Paper by the Department of External Affairs), 23 August 1957, p. 638.

simplicity and the way it became enmeshed in village life — still working as a village's principal source of safe water, and managed by local residents themselves.

By 2000, Australia was no longer seeking 'big-ticket' aid projects in Myanmar, and it was sometimes even difficult to ensure that Myanmar was included in Australia's capacity building programs with ASEAN well after Myanmar's admission into ASEAN in 1997. (Whenever Myanmar was included in such programs, it worked hard to ensure it was not a 'drag' on such regional programs because of its own backward arrangements.) Meanwhile, from the mid-1990s on, the Australian Embassy actively implemented a grass-roots assistance program for small-scale community projects, which were highly successful in their impacts, and were meticulously implemented by local groups across the country, including in areas where it was not always possible for diplomats to travel, such as Northern Chin State. The Direct Assistance Program (DAP) was the only program directly under the control of the embassy, rather than being run out of Canberra, and reports of some of its achievements made their way into AusAID annual reports. The Japanese and British embassies had similar schemes that had similar excellent results. But all of these community-based programs fell far short of helping Myanmar develop its national infrastructure and national institutions to the desired level.

3

Australian Ambassador
to Myanmar

I had never been to Myanmar, and knew relatively little about the country when I took up my position in May 2000. But some one-off contacts in the early 1990s might have been a foretaste of things to come. A delegation of Australia-based Burmese activists called on then Foreign Minister Senator Gareth Evans in 1995, while I was working as his senior advisor. They left a very positive impression: they were intelligent, reasonable, and spoke excellent English. Unlike some who called on the minister, they did not seek to use their meeting with him for their own publicity, although the Australian Government could do very little for them at that time. I was to meet some of them again during consultations that Australian ambassadors normally have before, during, and after their overseas postings.

A further one-off contact arose in 1995–96 during my work with Senator Gareth Evans, who — as an 'activist' foreign minister — tried to establish benchmarks for progress as guidelines for the international community's responses to liberalising steps made by the Myanmar military regime.[1] Almost no other members of the international community were interested in relaxing their sanctions

---

1   Gareth Evans's proposals were presented in confidential sessions of the 1995 ASEAN-Plus ministerial meeting, and mentioned only in general terms in his public statement to the meeting: 'We should make clear to that leadership that the region will respond in a measured and positive way to the benchmark steps it takes towards that reconciliation, but that those steps need to be taken.' See: gevans.org/speeches/old/1995/020895_evans_address_aseanpmc.pdf.

or 'engaging' more closely with the military regime at that stage, even though the policies — of trying to isolate the regime and backing a democracy movement that could only claim a single effective leader — were manifestly not working. On the other hand, the difficulties of advancing the concept of 'benchmarks', which seemed entirely logical, exposed me to some of the problems in encouraging Burma towards the goal of reconciliation. The 'benchmarks' were attacked from all sides, mostly for ideological or political reasons, as if the activist community wanted nothing less than complete capitulation by the military regime and its humiliation. The 'benchmarks' quickly disappeared from the international agenda; perhaps they were too complex, and politically unrealistic. At the very least, they were ahead of the times. But, much later, the indicators of genuine change or progress in Myanmar were much the same as those laid down by Gareth Evans; and the responses from the international community were also similar, although not really coordinated. So, with Myanmar/ Burma, ideas can be condemned, even if they are good ideas.

In contrast to these brief glimpses, the overall tone of my official pre-departure briefings was intended to lower any expectations that the posting to Burma had any chance of achieving results. With sanctions firmly in place, and scarcely questioned, most of the normal aspects of relations between two countries were not present or existed in a rudimentary state, or, worse, it was insisted that generally no ambitions were held for improving relations, or for Australia playing a distinctive role in politically influencing Myanmar. The main official pre-posting briefings I received in Canberra in April/May 2000 had a common central theme: Burma had been downgraded as a priority for Australian policy, and trade, investment, tourism, and education were not considered to be areas where relations could be developed or enhanced because of Australia's sanctions against the military regime, which had existed since 1988. The ambassador's role was apparently to maintain a presence only. The most senior DFAT officer with line responsibilities for Burma in the department was explicit: there should be no effort put into 'political reporting', the normal mainstay for policy officers. Curiously, this was reinforced by a recent Australian Government decision to downgrade Burma as a lower priority of intelligence interest for the main Australian intelligence community.

All of this proved to be quite unrealistic, of course, and demands from Canberra (or elsewhere) for information or assessments were received quite frequently, regardless of this 'downgraded' ranking of the Yangon post. (This system of ranking posts by their 'importance' seemed to disappear at a later stage.) Even at the time, the 'downgrading' of Burma seemed to contradict some quite specific Australian interests: Australian police and immigration officers were as interested as ever in Burma as a potential source of criminal or immigration violations. Moreover, later — perhaps in 2002 — analysts from Australia's Office of National Assessments (ONA) made brief visits to Yangon to follow up various questions in which they remained interested, as was their normal practice around the world. There was no indication from them that Burma/Myanmar was a much lower priority than before.

One useful meeting before my departure was with the highly competent and personable Myanmar Ambassador U Aye, who, as is sometimes the practice, kindly invited me to lunch. U Aye was one of Myanmar's best diplomats, going on later to be Ambassador to South Africa. Although I was not aware at the time, he had considerable experience working with Myanmar's military intelligence. He would later retire in Australia — as had some Burmese diplomats before him, and where his daughter had received her university education — and led a quiet life of seclusion. In Myanmar, his brother, U Myint, was a prominent economist who had worked at the Ministry of Foreign Affairs and later the UN Economic and Social Commission for Asia and the Pacific (ESCAP), and would later become an economic advisor to Aung San Suu Kyi and — in 2011 — to the reformist president, Thein Sein. Like previous Australian ambassadors, I got to know U Myint very well, and I met him quite often later whenever I returned to Myanmar.

In preparing to take up the position of ambassador, it was essential to consult members of the Burmese community in Australia, and members of the pro-democracy movement based in Australia. Not all members of the Burmese community in Australia were associated with the activist movement, which was represented mainly by the Burma Campaign Australia. Some, such as the Anglo-Burmans, who had migrated in the 1950s, and others who had come before (and sometimes after) the 1988 disturbances, did not wish to be involved in political activity. Certain ethnic groups did not like to mingle with others. So in my 'consultations' I usually needed to arrange several meetings with the Burmese community, rather than a single meeting.

The influence of the activist movement in Australia in support of the restoration of democracy in Myanmar was not as great as that in counterpart countries, such as the US and the UK. I met a number of their leaders during my briefings, and remained in occasional contact with Dr Myint Cho, one of the 1990 MPs resident in Australia, and undoubtedly their most effective public 'voice' in Australia.[2] There was a representative of, but never a formal office of, the government-in-exile in Australia, although some senior members of the National Coalition Government of the Union of Burma (NCGUB) were full- or part-time residents in Australia.[3] There was never an official representative of the National League for Democracy (NLD) in Australia, although some NLD supporters rather late in the piece declared themselves a 'liberated zone' — it is not clear whether they had any authority for this. It is hard to pinpoint the reasons for this lack of more visible support, but the difference in impact is — in hindsight — noticeable. Sympathy in response to the repression of Burmese democracy was certainly strong and consistent over time in Australia, and relatively large numbers of Burmese were accepted as refugees — across the main ethnic groups — and later as asylum seekers. But this did not translate into the sort of significant government policies one might have expected, despite many years of active lobbying for their cause. Why was this?

Australian Labor Party (ALP) support for the Burmese democracy movement was quite overt: the Australia Burma Council formerly had its office in the Sussex Street headquarters of the New South Wales (NSW) ALP.[4] But in the various parliaments around Australia, parliamentary groups supporting Burmese democracy went across party lines, and the minor parties — the Democrats and subsequently the Greens — have been particularly strong supporters. For example, at the federal level, Australian political parties resisted economic sanctions against the Burmese military regime until its response to the 'Saffron Revolution' in 2007, when financial sanctions were adopted and quickly won strong bipartisan support. But they did not last long. Australia was one of the first countries to suspend its economic

---

2   Members of the National Coalition Government of the Union of Burma Cabinet residing in Australia include Foreign Affairs Spokesman Teddy Buri, and Information Spokesman Daniel Aung. Dr Myint Cho was affiliated with the Australia–Burma Council.

3   Amanda Zappia was Australian representative of the NCGUB until February 2000, when she stepped down for personal reasons. She was never replaced as representative of the NCGUB, although other members of the Australia Burma Council acted as spokesmen.

4   The Burma Campaign Australia, successor to the Australia Burma Council, is located in the NSW Trade Hall building.

sanctions after political reforms progressed in Myanmar after 2011. Support for Burma's pro-democracy movement reached all Australian political parties and most parliaments, but core support was possibly split between the Australian Labor Party and the Greens. Some key members of the ALP were highly influential on Burma, but the ALP was not really the strong 'fraternal' party of the NLD that it might have been. Later, it was noticeable to me that Aung San Suu Kyi herself did not visit Australia until the end of 2013, three years after her release from house arrest.

The Burmese community in Australia was generally as committed as it could have been to democracy, and participated in every manner of community-based protest activity — such as mass rallies in capital cities and outside the Myanmar Embassy in Canberra — but some former MPs were under warrants for 'absconding' after the 1990 elections and adopted a low-key public profile. Support for democracy was, to a certain extent, fragmented across the Australian states, and some leading figures (such as those associated with the government-in-exile resident in Australia) spent a considerable amount of their time in Thailand. In other parts of the Australian community, however, support for democracy in Myanmar was not as directly connected to the NLD as elsewhere, although when Suu Kyi did visit Australia in late 2013, the crowds that came out and attended functions in her honour in Sydney, Canberra, and Melbourne were large and enthusiastic. Many members of the Burmese community were strongly apolitical, and preferred not involve themselves in political activism, especially if they were in the habit of visiting their families in Myanmar. Interestingly, the Myanmar Embassy in Canberra seemed to maintain contact with quite a wide range of Burmese residents of Australia, including some who no longer had Burmese citizenship.

The Australian trade union movement was always one of the strongest areas of support for the democracy cause in Myanmar, and the Australian Council of Trade Unions (ACTU)-affiliated organisation Australian People for Health, Education and Development Abroad (APHEDA) was one of the more effective Australian support groups.[5] While many Australian church groups were also very sympathetic,

---

5   According to APHEDA's website: 'Union Aid Abroad-APHEDA's international program has developed from a rights based approach. Our work aims to build self-reliance through support to educational and training projects for workers and their organisations. See: apheda.org.au.

their direct involvement seemed to be channelled through counterpart church groups and needy communities in Burma rather than through the NLD. Larger Australian humanitarian international non-governmental organisations (INGOs) focused very effectively on the humanitarian aspects of their work, both in fundraising in Australia and program delivery in Burma, rather than on seeking greater political support in Australia or Myanmar. Australian tourists — who might have provided some impetus for more assertive government policies — tended to stay away from Myanmar, preferring other Southeast Asian destinations until recent years.

The overall picture of Australian interest in the plight of the Burmese people is not clear-cut and is somewhat mixed. The thinking of the Australian media — particularly the national media such as the ABC and SBS — was considerably influenced by the pro-democracy cause, as was international media anywhere, which certainly contributed to greater awareness and sympathy among Australians generally. But the Australian media did not give prominence to any single representative of the activist community in Australia, which did not have a high-profile leader. However, Australian academics made some notable and distinctive contributions to the overall democracy cause, including some working directly with the NLD. Australians have probably been as sympathetic on the Rohingya problem as the international community anywhere. Australia has long been one of the main sources of humanitarian assistance for the Rohingya through international agencies such as the World Food Programme and the United Nations High Commissioner for Refugees (UNHCR). Another problem may have been that Australian support efforts were focused on the affected displaced Burmese on the border with Thailand — in refugee camps and the armed resistance — where progress arising from political changes inside Myanmar was slowest to materialise.

Reflecting this persistent downplaying of Australia's interests in Burma/Myanmar, the staffing levels of the Australian Embassy in Yangon were very modest. In particular, representatives of Australian Government departments in the Australian Embassy had been drastically reduced since 1988, and were confined to DFAT and the Australian Federal Police (and the latter only arrived in 1999, the year before I assumed my duties in the embassy). There was no representative from the Australian Agency for International Development (AusAID), which in 2013 reached eight Australia-based people. The defence attaché had long been withdrawn; the Australian Defence Attaché to Thailand was accredited to Myanmar from Bangkok and usually visited Yangon twice a year. The Austrade office consisted of one local staff officer, with a commercial counsellor from Austrade occasionally visiting from the Australian Embassy in Bangkok (although these visits became less and less frequent). Australian immigration staff from the Bangkok Embassy visited regularly for operational reasons, and in 2003 the Department of Immigration (unilaterally) offered the Myanmar Government training in detecting passport fraud, a problem that Australia took seriously and hoped to encourage regional authorities to pursue more systematically. The Myanmar Ministry of Immigration and Population — whose minister was, of course, a general — eventually accepted the offer, which was for them rather unusual and, at first blush, slightly surprising.

DFAT annual reports from between 1998 and 2002 illustrate how thin the official relationship was during this period, repeatedly referring euphemistically to 'carefully balanced' policy or 'carefully judged' approach. Despite the 1997 dispatch of Special Envoy John Dauth (the senior departmental officer responsible for Southeast Asia at the time) to make direct personal representations about Myanmar's need to pursue reforms, little hope was really held that such changes might occur. Thus, when Australian Foreign Minister Alexander Downer launched a human rights training initiative in 1999, it was always stated that the Australian Government did not expect the program would necessarily bring immediate or detectable improvements. Outside government-to-government relations, nothing else merited mention in DFAT's annual reports during this period. In a real sense, with or without direct Australian Government support, many projects and instances of Australia–Myanmar cooperation flourished. Sanctions did not stop all forms of (or desire for) collaboration. But it can hardly be said that relations were reaching their full potential.

The condition of the Chancery of the Australian Embassy on Strand Road in downtown Yangon was arguably another sign of the low priority Burma was being accorded by DFAT at this time. Just over $1 million had just been spent on a refurbishment of the fairly unpromising embassy building, which had formerly been an outbuilding of the famous Strand Hotel next door. While the building had some charm, it was not designed to be an embassy. An Australian contractor had been on site as foreman for the last part of the refurbishing project, but it seems to have been done 'on the cheap', and many problems remained after its supposed completion in 2000, especially in relation to 'rising damp' — exacerbated because no tropical-grade dehumidifying equipment had been installed in the air conditioning system. (The residual moisture in the ambassador's office was so high that a stalactite-like fungus began to grow out of a gap in the ceiling as soon as it was repainted.) Embassy staff patiently reported these problems to Canberra as they appeared, but we received little response, even when we pointed out the health implications for embassy staff. When we sent a report by cable listing the outstanding problems, we were admonished for showing lack of judgement. Yet less than five years later, DFAT was proposing to build a completely new chancery in Yangon on the grounds that the old (refurbished) one was 'no longer' suitable and 'no longer' complied with Australian health and safety standards.[6]

It is not necessarily unusual to discover a gap between the expectations of Canberra's bureaucracy — which normally compromised any ambassador's instructions — and the expectations that exist in the Australian community or in the country to which one is assigned. It would not normally be a good sign if this gap were too large. I knew of many instances in which an Australian ambassador had fought against limited or confining official guidelines issued from Canberra, but also knew that such situations could be professionally and personally detrimental. I was not really surprised when local expectations seemed quite a mismatch with my very unambitious official briefings, but on the whole managed to live with this, while always trying to ensure I informed Canberra clearly what any expectations were, whether or not they were welcome.

Coordination of policy with like-minded counterpart countries was an important part of the Australian Embassy role in Myanmar, but Australia's profile was not consistently in the front line. Australia had been a member of UN Special Envoy Alvaro de Soto's ill-fared 'Friends of Burma' group in 1998, but this group had become

---

6   In its submission to the Parliamentary Public Works Committee at the end of 2006, DFAT stated: 'Although extensively refurbished over the years, the chancery no longer satisfies security set-back, access, building services or efficient work space needs, or current Australian building code and occupational health and safety requirements. A purpose-built chancery will meet these requirements and provide an efficient and safe working environment.' Senate Hansard, 6 November 2006.

moribund by 2000. Australia was not invited to the Chilston Park meetings organised by the UK Government during 2001–02. However, Australia did participate in less-focused meetings of an informal Walker Hill (Seoul) group, and it proved most informative for me to attend one of these meetings alongside my predecessor as ambassador, Lyndall MacLean, in Seoul in early 2000. When UN Secretary-General Ban Ki Moon revived the 'Friends of Myanmar' group after 2007, Australia was again a participant. Whenever UN envoys visited Myanmar, Australia routinely attended the briefings provided at the end of their visits.

Australia's formal status in relation to such groups did not seem to matter much in Yangon, where we were still taken seriously by the Myanmar Government and by representatives of the international community with whom there was regular interaction. Australia was expected to participate in such arrangements involving regional countries; indeed, non-participation by Australia might even have been seen by some as a sign that Australia was not playing its part. In part, Australian participation in multilateral consultations arose directly from Australia's role as a regular donor to the relevant international agencies — United Nations Development Programme (UNDP), UNICEF, UNHCR, World Health Organization (WHO), etc. Between 2000–03, Australia only played a leading role in one multilateral program, namely the so-called 'Mini-Dublin Group' of the UN Office of Drugs and Crime (then United Nations International Drug Control Programme (UNDCP)). By convention, Australia and Japan took it in turns to chair the monthly meetings of this group, although much of the initiative for setting the agenda remained with UNDCP. The main Australian initiative on the ground during this period was to invite the Myanmar Police Force to provide an advance briefing for the group on the Myanmar Government's proposed money laundering legislation. At this time, it was still rare for the home government, Myanmar, to participate in such multilateral consultations in Yangon.

It was not apparent to me that whatever role Australia played was the product of a deliberate or specific strategy by Canberra. We rarely received specific briefing from Canberra for these meetings, and did not often receive routine background information that might have been relevant. Despite the value of any information sharing and policy consultation that occurred, it is hard even now to point to these groups as a source of major initiatives or breakthroughs, although they certainly performed less ambitious roles quite well, and occasionally got the ear of the military regime. One constant problem with these consultative groups was that the military regime was never represented, so the meetings inevitably created an 'us and them' atmosphere, and the military regime never felt unduly pressured to take them seriously; or, to put it differently, the military regime could hardly have been said to have anything to fear from these groups. It goes without saying that Myanmar opposition groups were not party to any of these discussions, although some Western countries (such as the US and the UK) may have consulted Aung San Suu Kyi and her party separately.

Australian ambassadors normally have an opportunity to refresh their working strategies with Canberra by returning to Australia for mid-term 'leave and consultations'. Mine were due to occur around the end of 2001, but as a federal election was scheduled for November 2001, all leave and consultations by our ambassadors overseas were deferred, and my mid-term consultations eventually occurred in February 2002. This was very useful, as it enabled two-way conversations about the expectations of our Yangon Embassy, although from memory it was more valuable for me for the additional opportunities to interact with Australian and Burmese 'constituencies' in Australia than for any new or substantial adjustment to my official briefings. I remember discussing the 60th anniversary of the Burma–Thailand Railway with the Department of Veterans Affairs and the Returned and Services League, who both very reasonably indicated they would be responsive to the level of public interest in the anniversary to determine what official involvement would be appropriate. (The then Director of the Australian War Memorial, Gary Beck, encouraged me to see if it would be possible to acquire an engine from the Burma–Thailand Railway for their collection.)

4

Working Under Military Authoritarian Rule

Official day-to-day dealings between Yangon embassies and the military regime in Myanmar involved a good measure of pragmatism on both sides. In effect, this represented routine dealings with the government that was in effective control. Nobody ever suggested this implied any degree of consent or condoning of Myanmar's military regime. The job of all diplomats everywhere is to build up networks of well-informed, independent, accessible, and reliable contacts inside and outside the host government, among political parties, opposition groups, and NGOs, so that they can report objectively, accurately, and in a timely way to their home governments on all manner of topics. Myanmar was no different, but the fact that it operated as a police state, with a highly visible and basically hostile intelligence service, presented some obvious problems. In the early 2000s, when the local people's movements and activities were closely monitored by their own government, it could be very difficult to gather information, although it is now much easier to do this in Myanmar. After I left Myanmar in 2003, I was able, even then, to remain in touch with some of my most valuable contacts through the internet, and through my occasional visits to Myanmar.

Australia maintained a very small embassy in Yangon: in 2000–03, we only had six Australia-based staff from DFAT and one officer from the Australian Federal Police (AFP), who had been assigned to Yangon in 1999.[1] Working as an Australian diplomat in Myanmar at this time was interesting, sometimes challenging, and occasionally one encountered the unexpected. Any government maintaining an embassy in Yangon at this time accepted that this would in itself bring them into direct contact with the military regime. So there was no point in having scruples about dealing directly with a 'pariah regime'. Some Western governments chose not to maintain an embassy for this reason, while others, such as European Union (EU) members and Australia, chose not to develop military-to-military cooperation with the regime, and, to underline this, decided not to station a defence attaché in their embassy. Even this did not mean ceasing all contact with the military as such, because, as in Australia's case, defence attachés accredited from Bangkok could still visit Myanmar for occasions such as Armed Forces Day (held annually on 27 March), when the military regime organised a formal program for the visiting attachés. It was not clear that this very limited contact brought worthwhile results, other than allowing a few Australian military officers to become a little familiar with the Burmese Army. Of course, all Australian Embassy staff were constantly watchful for any attempt by the military regime to take advantage of their enormous police powers; this included being on the alert for signs that Australian or Myanmar Embassy staff were subject to any form of pressure or were in any way vulnerable. While this meant staff had to cope with more stress than would normally be the case, both at work and outside the office, these were understood as the conditions we had to live under. We assumed that all foreign diplomatic staff were under surveillance.

The martial law regime (SLORC/SPDC) established as a result of the 1988 coup had at least a public or 'in principle' commitment to handing over power to a 'multi-party democracy' after holding national elections. Arguably, the military regime would have ended much sooner if the NLD had not walked out of the National Convention in 1995, thereby leaving the whole constitutional process in a state of suspense until 2005. (The army could have resumed the National Convention process much sooner if they wanted to, and as they eventually did, but they must have hoped for NLD to return to the process earlier, albeit in

---

1   By contrast, in 2013, there was a big AusAID section, plus the AFP office, and a trade commissioner (appointed earlier in the year); by the start of 2014, a defence attaché also arrived, bringing the Australian official representation back to something like it was in 1988, 25 years earlier.

a subordinate role. The army never were any good at negotiations.) Inside the country, however, many still blame the NLD for making a strategic mistake when they walked out in 1995 — and again when they refused to participate in the elections held under that constitution in 2010.

Burma had been a centrally planned state since the 1960s. While the country was definitely under quite effective military rule in 2000, it still possessed a substantial bureaucracy, including a large number of experienced technocrats in areas in which the state traditionally played a leading role, such as education, health, and agricultural support. Although this meant a very large number of civilians were working as civil servants, they were always under strong military control, through having generals openly working (in uniform) as deputy ministers and in other leading positions, as well as a sprinkling of military officers throughout the ministries (often working in plain clothes). The civilian bureaucracy had some patches of technical competence,[2] but not any flair or innovativeness — and certainly not any ability to take on 'risk'.[3] Lack of effective authority had long been a major weakness in the bureaucracy, dating back to Ne Win times. Moreover, Burmese officials were not permitted to criticise the military regime, and were certainly not allowed to express support for the NLD and Aung San Suu Kyi.

However, the army did not necessarily regard itself as the natural ruling party, even though it had long been groomed for a 'nation-building' role going well beyond preserving national unity and national security. In regional areas, for example, the local military commander also served as the regional governor, with de facto responsibility for all administration, with both soldiers and civilians (for example, from the General Affairs Department of the Ministry of Home Affairs) under his authority. In the early 2000s, army colleges offered the first MBAs in Myanmar, and civil administration still features in their curricula. Yet, most of the population regarded the army as incapable of running the country competently. (The official response to Cyclone Nargis in 2008 provided compelling evidence for

---

2   Visiting Australian technical people would occasionally comment positively to me on the technical knowledge of officials in health, agriculture, and civil engineering.

3   The best description of the Burmese state at this time is David Steinberg's *Burma: The State of Myanmar*, Washington DC: Georgetown University Press, 2001.

the people's assessment.) On the other hand, the Burmese generals dismissed politicians — including the NLD — as incapable of running the country. Senior military members of the regime, as well as the regime's own propaganda, constantly reminded people that the regime was committed to relinquishing power, even though many of its actions to suppress dissent by force (in 1996 and 2007, as well as 1988) might have suggested otherwise.

Although in many respects the Burmese army is not necessarily regarded highly by the people, and while to some extent it has developed its own separate socio-economic institutions (hospitals, universities), on the whole the army is an institution that is integrated into society: there have long been retired army people working across the bureaucracy, and this might become even more common as the army downsizes if and when insurgency ends; and many families would have one son who volunteered for the army (though this can lead to a breakdown in family relationships). There is no strong 'us and them' division between the army and the people. Although the army is — consistently — a source of human rights abuses and mistreatment of people, and is already widely blamed for many of the country's problems, it is also acknowledged as one of the few strong national institutions that has historically made great contributions to the formation of the state. There is no doubt, however, that by around 2000 the army was universally regarded as not competent to be the government, and was seriously mismanaging the country by its socio-economic policies. In many quarters, the army was despised, profoundly distrusted, and looked down on. All levels of Burmese society openly made jokes at the expense of the army, and directed at Than Shwe personally, which demonstrated that the army no longer enjoyed widespread popular support as a national institution.

On the other hand, while the Burmese Army naturally used any limited contacts it had with Australian entities to present itself in the best light, and to win some sympathy from their Australian counterparts, to my knowledge they made no attempt to exploit normal commercial contacts in unacceptable ways. Occasionally, Australian companies sent representatives to Myanmar to explore possible commercial opportunities. Sometimes these 'opportunities' involved dealing with the military regime or its state-owned enterprises, but the Australian Embassy could not be involved in assisting such efforts, and during my time in Myanmar the embassy was not involved. Knowing this, around this time only a small number of Australian companies ever visited Myanmar in search of commercial opportunities. At the same time, it was assumed that the Burmese Army could be seeking to import dual-use (civilian/military) equipment from Australia.

Khin Nyunt's Office of Strategic Studies: Agent of or façade for change?

The main 'face' of the SPDC/SLORC was Secretary One, Lieutenant-General Khin Nyunt, who was, in effect, Chief Cabinet Secretary and the regime's spokesman, and who could deal with all issues for all audiences. Formally, Khin Nyunt was head of the military intelligence organisation in the Burmese Army. He had advanced quite quickly through the ranks, but rightly or wrongly was always regarded as lacking front-line operational experience and support. He was seen as highly intelligent and articulate, and the international media portrayed him as being 'moderate' and reform minded. He was also seen as the driving force behind the regime's limited attempts at opening up the country.[4] Under Khin Nyunt, Myanmar's military intelligence (generally known as 'MI') had a reputation for efficiency, ruthlessness, and (relative) openness. It had its staff placed in all arms of government, and had gathered a group of well educated, confident, and articulate officers with some experience of foreign countries, who accepted their intermediary role in bringing peace to Myanmar, both internally and externally. It was Khint Nyunt's staff that had negotiated and consummated ceasefire agreements with 17 ethnic groups between 1989 and 2000. They also controlled counter-narcotics policies though the government's Central Committee on Drug Abuse Control (CCDAC), and all aspects of internal security.

By 2000, it was widely accepted that Khin Nyunt had created his own 'change agency' inside the military intelligence organisation that he headed. Although called the 'Office of Strategic Studies' (OSS),[5] it was not an 'office' in the sense of being a separate or independent body;

---

4   Some of his thinking was evident in his interviews with journalists at the time, such as one by *China Express*: www.burmafund.org/Research_Library/interview_with_khin_nyunt.htm.

5   An excellent description of how the Office of Strategic Studies functioned can be found in Andrew Selth's seminal work *Burma's Armed Forces: Power Without Glory*, Norwalk, Connecticut: EastBridge, 2002.

it was staffed entirely by military intelligence officers who worked on both domestic and international policies under their leader Major-General Kyaw Win, Khin Nyunt's close associate.[6] It had specific responsibilities for international relations, anti-narcotics policy, and ethnic affairs, where its authority exceeded that of the line government agencies. Importantly, it also had chief responsibility as the liaison channel for the dialogue with Aung San Suu Kyi, through Major-General Kyaw Win and other senior OSS officers. OSS staff tended to be well educated, had good policy skills, and spoke good English, and they were noticeably comfortable, indeed confident, in dealing with foreigners. Their military status was quite overt, and they were open about their lines of command. Among embassies, they came to be regarded as the best people to get problems 'fixed'. They were almost alone among anyone in the SPDC regime in having contact with Aung San Suu Kyi and being prepared to discuss her.

Khin Nyunt was de facto prime minister long before he was given the formal title in 2003. He was extremely competent, decisive, and demonstrably familiar with a wide range of policy issues. He spoke reasonably good English and understood it quite well, although (sensibly) when conducting formal business, he would use an interpreter. In person, Khin Nyunt was impressive and reasonable, although he could be tough and even ruthless, and was a formidable negotiator. He took his responsibilities seriously and seemed to enjoy his power and his role thoroughly. People recognised that he wielded enormous authority and that he could be counted on to deal with complex problems and any political issues that arose. It was accepted that he was prepared to take risks, and to consider new and unprecedented approaches. His leadership encouraged the international community to see him as showing a way forward. Burmese people were always conscious of his capacity to exercise the authority of a dictatorship. At this time, Khin Nyunt seemed to be domestically and internationally regarded as the military leader who might be able to lead the country towards national reconciliation, and who might be able to persuade the more conservative regime head, Senior General Than Shwe, to go along with some changes. While this might have been an optimistic scenario, it seemed to enjoy some

---

6   Major-General Kyaw Win was an extremely intelligent and affable military commander, and also quite an accomplished amateur painter. He was called on from time to time to 'negotiate' with Aung San Suu Kyi.

credibility even among members of the military, although senior ministers and generals often mentioned regretfully their inability to convince the top leaders of the virtues of new policies.

The Office of Strategic Studies was in many ways the international face of the military regime and, compared to some other parts of the Myanmar Government, was relatively accessible. At one level, OSS managed the regime's public relations; at another level they controlled dealings with the outside world, including foreign visa and Myanmar passport issue.[7] On arrival in Yangon, it was normal to pay an initial courtesy call on OSS, as well as on other ministries. Like all military organisations, they were relatively formal and protocol-conscious, but they were reasonably friendly and gave the impression of being helpful. All embassies in Yangon adopted a pragmatic approach to dealing with the OSS and military intelligence.[8] The bureaucracy and OSS were relatively open about the roles that each played, but this sometimes meant leaders of the mainstream army were not involved in many of the day-to-day affairs of state. Civilian parts of the Myanmar Government bureaucracy did not necessarily enjoy being overshadowed by military intelligence, but some bureaucrats seemed to work very closely — if not always comfortably — with military intelligence staff. Khin Nyunt and his deputy, Major-General Kyaw Win, were generally impressive and competent, and their senior colleagues, Brigadier-General Thein Swe and Brigadier-General Kyaw Thein (on narcotics and ethnic issues), were also cooperative and efficient. Ultimately, OSS staff tended to be somewhat cocky and perhaps over-confident in their role, and this may be why they were a particular target for the purge that happened in 2004–05.

The OSS could be extremely helpful, especially in handling slightly unusual situations, as its staff were less hidebound than the bureaucracy, had the authority to overrule the bureaucracy, and knew that they would not be challenged if they obtained Khin Nyunt's blessing for any proposed action. They were often an avenue of last resort for foreign embassies. On one occasion, the Australian Embassy in its consular role needed to contact an Australian backpacker who

---

7   In 2000, the regime's official spokesman, Lieutenant Colonel Hla Min, wrote a propaganda publication for the regime entitled 'Political Situation of Myanmar and its Role in the Region', which is now in its 26th edition.

8   Of course, Western embassies also considered Burma's military intelligence to be a 'hostile' intelligence service, and the necessary security protections were used.

was travelling 'up country' and we asked military intelligence if they could help us locate the young man to tell him that his father was seriously ill in Australia. Military intelligence obliged and, eventually, some time later (too late, as it happened) provided us with detailed list of where the young man had travelled and the hotels he had stayed in. The only problem was that the information reached the Australian Embassy long after the young man had returned to Australia. This anecdote reveals several sides of Burma's military intelligence: their wide reach that could be quite effectively targeted; their extreme technological backwardness; and their readiness to provide assistance in some circumstances.

Dealings with the Army

Protocol demanded that the Australian Ambassador present credentials to the Commander-in-Chief, Senior General Than Shwe, who was head of the military regime (the State Peace and Development Council), and to make introductory and farewell calls on the de facto prime minister, General Khin Nyunt. It was also not unusual to see General Khin Nyunt at national day receptions of leading Asian countries.

Embassies had little or no contact with Commander-in-Chief, Senior General Than Shwe, other than in the case of high-level visits, such as the October 2002 visit of Australian Foreign Minister Alexander Downer to Myanmar, which included a courtesy call on Than Shwe in his capacity as head of state. Than Shwe would occasionally be seen from a distance at formal state occasions. There was even less contact with former head of state, Ne Win, who was living under de facto house arrest in a remote location on the edge of Inya Lake in Yangon. Members of the public and foreigners were not permitted to meet Ne Win, although members of his family (his children) were occasionally in contact with some senior Burmese. Although Ne Win was reputed to be pulling the strings behind the military regime, there was no evidence whatsoever of this by 2000: no verified reports of interaction between Ne Win and the military leadership; no reports of any kind of interventions by Ne Win in policies, politics, or national security matters; no rumours or anecdotal reports of Ne Win's satisfaction or dissatisfaction with the state of the nation. In hindsight, it seemed that promoting stories of Ne Win retaining real power suited conspiracy theorists, and those who sought to discredit the Than Shwe/Khin Nyunt leadership of the army. In fact, whether he did or did not retain political influence made no difference at all. When Ne Win finally died in December 2002, the military regime even denied him an official funeral, more or less confirming that he had long lost any standing.[9] There were no observable consequences from his death.

As an embassy without a military attaché on its staff in-country, the Australian Embassy, like many other embassies, had almost no direct dealings at all with uniformed officers in the one organisation that ran Myanmar, the Burmese Army, or *Tatmadaw*. The only immediate consequence of this was that, as ambassador of a country that did not have a defence attaché on its embassy staff, and did not maintain active defence relations, I did not receive an invitation to attend the Burmese Army's annual Armed Forces Day celebrations. (This is not to say that this event was without its impact on anyone living in Yangon: with a large parade of soldiers, and some equipment, near the centre of the city, and rehearsals for weeks before and — even by 2003 — live television coverage on the day, one could not be unaware of the event.)

As in some other countries where access to the government was not easy, quite a bit of business would be transacted with Myanmar Government leaders attending national day receptions. I recall one diplomatic reception, before the 40th anniversary of the Burma–Thailand Railway in 2002, at which I tackled General Khin Nyunt over the very poor state of the road between Yangon and Mawlamyaing, by which elderly Australian former POWs would have to travel in order to attend the commemorative event at Thanbyuzayat (just south of Mawlamyaing) in May 2003. I was concerned that some of our veteran visitors might suffer health problems because of the state of the road. It was probably not normal, and certainly not encouraged, for ambassadors to raise such negative and possibly embarrassing issues with army leaders. Foreign Minister U Win Aung (now deceased) pulled at my arm to drag me away from General Khin Nyunt, who listened but did not make any very specific commitment to me. But some repair work was subsequently done on the road before the railway anniversary event. It was perhaps planned to occur anyway.

---

9   The Reuters report of his death, compiled with input from the Reuters stringer in Yangon, can be seen at: www.dawn.com/news/70684/ne-win-dies-at-91.

At this time, there were perhaps only four ministers in the cabinet who were not from the army,[10] so meetings with any other ministers were with army generals. The sports minister who attended the 2000 Olympic Games in Sydney with the Myanmar athletes was Brigadier-General Aye Win. His attendance required a waiver of the travel bans applied by Australia against the military regime. The travel bans had a significant effect in deterring high-level official travel to Australia, which was not always for the public good. We had only one clear example where the bans were applied when it might have been beneficial if the visit had proceeded. This was a proposed visit by the Mayor of Mandalay, who was attracted by some traffic light technology being manufactured and exported by an Australian company in Melbourne, and was planning to visit with an eye to consummating the purchase. When it was realised he was a brigadier-general, his proposed visit was aborted, and his visa application was denied, and as far as I know the sale did not proceed. So the commercial returns were lost by the Australian firm, and Mandalay would have obtained its traffic lights from another source. Slightly lower-level military officers of the rank of colonel or lieutenant colonel were permitted (by special arrangement) to attend an ASEAN Regional Forum meeting in Sydney in 2002.

Of course, embassies also dealt routinely with those military officers who held ministerial rank in the cabinet/government — whose rank ranged from major-general to colonel. These ministers wore their uniform proudly when working inside Myanmar, but would attend international meetings in other countries in civilian clothes. One also encountered uniformed officers in their regional commander roles, when travelling 'up country'. In my case, I had occasion to call on the Deputy Regional Commander in Rakhine State for a briefing on the security situation there. I also called on the Regional Commander in Mon State to seek his cooperation in a broad sense for Australian participation in the 2003 anniversary of the Burma–Thailand Railway. However, embassies did not normally have dealings with the military

---

10   U Soe Tha, the Minister for National Planning and Economic Development (elected in 2010 as a Union Solidarity and Development Party MP and Committee Chair in the People's Assembly); U Than Aung, the Minister for Education (now deceased); David Abel, the Minister for Trade (a former military officer, now retired); and Dr Kyaw Myint, Health Minister after 2001 (now retired).

corporations — Union of Myanmar Economic Holdings or Myanmar Economic Corporation — or any of the other military arms of the Ministry of Defence, the three services (army, navy, and air force).

The major military event on the annual calendar was Armed Services Day, 27 March, which was usually an occasion for a massive march by army troops, but not necessarily for displays of military hardware, as in some other countries. Streets in Yangon were closed off for this event, and for the rehearsals that took place in the weeks leading up to 27 March. The Australian Defence Attaché (from Bangkok) usually attended this event, but no other Australian embassy staff were invited to attend. So the Australian Ambassador and other staff had almost no opportunity or occasion to get to know regular members of the military. (By contrast, the US Chargé d'Affaires in Yangon often played golf with senior military officers, thanks partly to the connections the US Government maintained with the *Tatmadaw* through the three US military attachés stationed in their embassy in Myanmar, notwithstanding US sanctions.) The absence of regular, direct, and effective channels of communication with the military was undoubtedly something of a handicap, but it did not really produce problems for the Australian Embassy at this time. Defence attaché visits from Bangkok were a useful supplement for our limited defence intelligence needs, but their necessarily infrequent and occasional character meant they did not seem to lead to significant deeper understanding of the military regime.[11] This may have changed a few years later when a successor defence attaché in Bangkok found his visit more productive.

The one regular contact the Australian Embassy had with the army was to request them to provide a bugler for the annual Anzac Day service, which was held at the Yangon Commonwealth War Cemetery on 25 April.[12] They regularly did this, and indeed seemed be to be pleased to oblige. Since Burma was still a colony and not independent in World War II, remembrance of World War II military history was not as

---

11   Politically, at this time, with almost no sign of flexibility on the part of the military about transferring political power, it would not have been realistic for Australia to seek to engage more directly with members of the military.

12   Only seven Australian soldiers are buried in the Yangon Cemetery, compared to some 23 at the largest Commonwealth War Cemetery at Taukkyant, north of Yangon, and 1,350 prisoner of war graves at the Commonwealth War Cemetery for the Burma–Thailand Railway at Thanbyuzayat (see Chapter 10).

prominent in Myanmar as one might have expected, given the country was directly ruled by the military from 1988–2011, and the small but valuable role the Burmese army played in victory over the Japanese in World War II. So Anzac Day and Remembrance Day (11 November) ceremonies were mainly attended by the foreign community, and any role the Burmese army played in these commemorations would not have been noticed by other Burmese. The Myanmar Government played no official part in these ceremonies at all.

In the early 2000s, the role of the Burmese army in controlling the country was not normally much in evidence. Large military barracks were a common sight around the country, but military troops were rarely seen in an operational role. Troops were deployed to border areas for military operations, but it was not common to see military troops stationed on the streets in Yangon or other major cities. This was somewhat surprising given that a military regime was running the country. If there were security alerts (for example, against a possible *coup d'état*) troops would sometimes be mobilised discreetly around town, usually overnight, and not in obvious view. Army leaders seemed intent on keeping their visible presence to a minimum, other than in their roles as ministers in the government when they customarily wore their military uniforms, and when they were often photographed. Even so, it was impossible for any foreigner living or working in Myanmar to be oblivious of the army.[13] At the same time, the fundamental role that the Burmese army has always played in Myanmar means that its unstated presence in the background is a factor that Burmese people live with, often uncomfortably. Moreover, this presence reaching right across the country could sometimes affect daily affairs, especially the affairs of Myanmar families, quite directly. Most embassies in Yangon paid close attention to the views and thinking of the military, to the extent that it was possible to ascertain what these were.

The modest commercial or non-governmental presence of Australian organisations and individuals in Myanmar did not bring them into much direct contact with the military. So, after 2000, the Australian Embassy had little cause to deal with the Burmese army on its own. This also meant we had little or no opportunity to influence the

---

13   Mary Callahan explains the often contradictory role of the army in state-building in *Making Enemies: War and State Building in Burma*, Singapore: Singapore University Press, 2004.

Burmese army, but this was not a role we were seeking, then or now.[14] After Australia's other sanctions against Myanmar were lifted between 2010 and 2012, the restrictions on direct cooperation with the military were retained. This reflects an enduring political constraint, whereby the pro-democracy advocates on Burma in Australia, as elsewhere, still criticise any direct Australian Government military dealings with the Burmese Army, and are reluctant to accept that such dealings could be justified, given the Burmese Army's continuing record of human rights abuses.

Ultimately, the Burmese Army is a highly secretive organisation, not given to making public statements to advertise or defend its policies. It was suspicious of outsiders, and distrusted foreigners as well as civilian Burmese.[15] At the same time, it was an extremely proud organisation, certain of its central place in holding the Myanmar state together, and assured about the absolute importance of its role in supporting national security. Aung San Suu Kyi was inclined to say that she accepted that the army would play a key role in nation-building, and was confident that they could more than hold their own against Thailand. However, after 1994, as the army spent less time fighting insurgency following the conclusion of various ceasefire agreements, its military prowess began to erode, and during the short border disagreement with Thailand in 2002 it lost out in cross-border skirmishes with Thai troops for the first time.

Working in a Police State

Anyone living in Myanmar in those days, even as a diplomat, was very conscious that Burma was a fairly effective police state, but its police state system also had some obvious weaknesses. It still relied mainly on paper documents; the IT age had not arrived fully

---

14   However, Dr John Blaxland from the Strategic and Defence Studies Centre at ANU, and Defence Attaché to Myanmar (and Thailand) from 2008–10, has argued that Australia could play a key role in influencing the *Tatmadaw* positively in regard to reform and ongoing state-building activities. See: John Blaxland, 'Myanmar: Time for Australian Defence Cooperation', *Security Challenges,* Vol. 7 No. 4, Summer 2011, pp. 63–76. Available at: www.regionalsecurity.org.au/Resources/Files/vol7no4Blaxland.pdf.
15   An Australian scholar specialising in the Burmese military, Dr Andrew Selth (who was formerly a diplomatic member of the Australian Embassy staff) still has professional contact with the military.

in Myanmar, so the regime's information was often incomplete, its communications arrangements were primitive, and its responses were not always timely. Nevertheless, one could not really escape the feeling of being regularly monitored, if not actually followed, and it was uncomfortable knowing that Burmese staff at the embassy or the ambassador's residence were probably reporting to military intelligence on one's activities. This meant one was always careful and automatically cautious in whatever one did.

One or the more irksome manifestations of the military regime was the tight control that was exercised, quite effectively, over in-country travel by the staff of foreign embassies and international agencies. For diplomats, it was necessary to obtain permission for any travel (private or official) more than 50 miles outside Yangon (other than for tourist trips to Pagan and Mandalay). One irritating aspect of this was that permission would always be granted at the last minute. In reciprocity, the Australian Government (like its Western counterparts) imposed parallel restrictions on Myanmar diplomats in Canberra. These travel restrictions mostly had a strong 'nuisance value'; I have never seen any study, official or otherwise, that demonstrated that these travel restrictions ever produced any other useful results. They were accepted as one of the array of security counter-measures (perhaps even 'counter-espionage' measures) against such governments. There was no formal effort made by either side to change or moderate this policy in this period.

The Australian Embassy operated under instructions from Canberra to comply with such restrictions. Personally, whenever possible, I avoided seeking permission to travel to areas where tourists were permitted to travel freely, and where diplomats should have been absolutely free to travel. But if I had reasons — official or otherwise — to travel to more unusual places, I normally 'notified' the Foreign Ministry; I specifically did not seek 'permission', although the ministry often responded formally by saying my travel had been 'approved'. I only rarely omitted to notify my intention to travel outside Yangon, and sometimes this did not seem to be noticed by the Myanmar authorities. It was sometimes possible to go to unusual parts of the country that were not generally 'open'. For example, permission was given for me to make an official visit to Northern Chin State in December 2002 so that we could inspect an embassy community aid project — a village water supply and mini-hydro scheme — that had been funded under the embassy's Direct Assistance Program. In early 2003, I joined an ASEAN ambassadors' tour of the famous ruby-mining area of Mogok, which was normally 'off-limits' for foreigners, presumably because of the risk of smuggling rubies, and perhaps because of the appalling working conditions of the miners.[16] There were few if any instances where an embassy or an ambassador was singled out by the Myanmar authorities for more favourable treatment under these arrangements. We never inquired about how the Chinese or (then) Soviet embassies were restricted.

In my case, travel permission was only denied twice. The first instance was when we sought to go further along the track of the World War II Burma–Thailand Railway — from Thanbyuzayat (the site of the Commonwealth War Cemetery) to Three Pagodas Pass — than had previously been allowed. Permission was denied on the grounds of security, which was slightly plausible, in that the New Mon State Army controlled territory there. (I am not aware of any foreigner being permitted to travel to Three Pagodas Pass from Thanbyuzayat until Professor Joan Beaumont from ANU in February 2013.) The leading ethnic group in the area, the New Mon State Party (NMSP), would normally have been prepared to allow travel within their territory, but their relations with the government were not good at this time. I encountered them only at road checkpoints where their territorial control began, although the NMSP sent an unofficial representative to the 60th anniversary ceremony we held at the Thanbyuzayat Commonwealth War Cemetery in 2003. On another occasion, my wife and I wanted to visit Laiza, the lacquerware production site in Shan state, privately, but we were told that on security grounds we could not go there. (There was some insurgent activity in the area, so this could have been a genuine reason.) I did not hear of any other foreigners visiting Laiza at this time.

Generally, during this period the authorities relaxed their restrictions on foreigners' travel quite considerably, and organisations such as the International Committee of the Red Cross (ICRC) were permitted to establish branch offices in a number of regional centres (some of which were later closed). During my three years in Yangon, I was able to travel widely around the country, mixing business and pleasure

---

16   All such officially approved tours were very tightly controlled during this period, with itineraries and meetings under strict Myanmar official restrictions.

(tourism), from the north in Kachin State, where Australian aid funds were going to the INGO World Concern, to the far south in Myeik, where the West Australian firm Atlantic Pearls had a joint venture with the Ministry of Mines. I was able to visit environmental sites (such as the Moyingyi Wetlands, listed under Ramsar),[17] cultural sites such as Pagan (later accepted for World Heritage listing by UNESCO), Sri Ksetra, the ancient archaeological Pyu site in Central Myanmar, and Mrauk-U in Rakhine State, as well as beach resorts (such as Ngwesaung, where development was overwhelmingly by private entrepreneurs). Only once, when trekking from Kalaw in Shan State to Inle Lake, was I directly affected by being followed by the security authorities, who tried to find me at the wrong hotel in Nyaung Shwe, at the northern end of Inle Lake, and loudly abused our tour guide — not in my presence — for misleading them (when it was plainly their mistake). When travelling by car along the track of the World War II Burma–Thailand Railway in Mon State, we eventually reached a security checkpoint beyond which we were not permitted to travel. Unlike my predecessor, I was allowed to visit Northern Chin State (Tiddim) to inspect an Australian aid project for a village water supply. I was only rarely conscious of being monitored or trailed by Myanmar security/intelligence vehicles, which were mostly unobtrusive, but our private driver sometimes openly reported our movements on these trips to MI staff. Several trips were organised by UN agencies such as UNICEF or UNHCR, for which Australia was a significant donor, both for Myanmar programs as well as more broadly.

Under existing standard procedures, as ambassador, I was required to obtain written permission from both Canberra and the Myanmar Government for any travel I undertook inside Myanmar, whether the travel was official or private. Securing approval from DFAT to undertake travel was not normally a problem, as long as the Embassy Number Two, the First Secretary, remained in Yangon. Obtaining permission from the Myanmar authorities in time to make the necessary logistical arrangements was not always easy, and once or twice when travelling to Mandalay or Pagan for tourism, I did not bother to seek their approval (on the grounds that foreign tourists did

---

17 Ramsar is the Convention on Wetlands of International Importance. Myanmar only ratified the convention in 2005, and Moyingi is Myanmar's only listed wetlands site. When I visited, preparations for its listing under Ramsar were already well advanced. See: www.ramsar.org/wetland/myanmar.

not need to obtain permission to travel to such sites). There were no consequences from this. I was given permission for all other trips, and travelled without any official 'escort' or security presence; other than a trip in early 2003 to Chin State, which was not open for tourists at that stage. On that trip to Northern Chin State (Haka, Tiddim, and Falang), I was obliged to accept two armed soldiers for security protection (although it was not certain that their weapons had bullets). There was no problem in following our planned itinerary and we were able to carry out our program as proposed. Needless to say, there was never any hint of a security problem. On none of my travels did I experience any 'incidents' or interference of any kind. Other than the trip to Chin State, I never sought permission from the Myanmar authorities to meet specific Myanmar individuals, many of whom worked for non-government bodies, while on these trips. If there were any concerns on the part of the Department of Foreign Affairs in Canberra on the grounds of security or anything else, they were never made known to me.

Whatever the extent to which our movements were monitored by the internal security authorities, I was never conscious of Myanmar non-government people in the regions being reluctant to meet me or fearful of the consequences of talking to me. At the same time, I did not seek to introduce political overtones into regional trips. Like other Western colleagues, I met former political prisoner and NLD-elected MP U Ohn Maung whenever we stayed at his Inle Princess Resort on Inle Lake in Shan State. There seemed to be no consequences from these meetings for U Ohn Maung, who spoke frankly about his experiences and his openly (but predictably) anti-government views. Most of the Myanmar people I met were cautious in their remarks, the notable exception being the rickshaw driver in Mawlamyaing who was quite happy to expound his fierce determination to run for the elections, while standing next to me in the middle of the road. When travelling inside Myanmar, I did not normally seek to meet regional Myanmar Government representatives, who were also regional military commanders. I usually had no business to raise with them, and to meet them could have implied inappropriate recognition of their political legitimacy. There were only two exceptions to this: when I called on the (Military) Governor of Mon State in early 2003 to alert him to the visit by Australian former prisoners of war to Thanbyuzayat, south of Mawlamyaing, for the 60th anniversary of the Burma–Thailand

Railway in May 2003; and when I called on the Deputy Regional Commander/Deputy Governor in Sittwe to explain Australia's interest in the plight of the Muslim Rohingya, as the largest foreign donor to the World Food Programme, and to urge the Myanmar Government to treat these people more reasonably. Not surprisingly, I was given the standard response by the Deputy Governor, who was some years later 'promoted' to be a deputy minister in the central government.

Pragmatic interaction with the government in effective control

The Australian Embassy had no specific detailed instructions on how to handle day-to-day dealings with the military regime. This would normally be left to the common sense judgement of embassy officers, and the absence of detailed guidelines was not really problematic. A pragmatic approach generally made sense. But the arms-length relationship that Australian governments preferred, for domestic political reasons, to maintain with the military regime could lead to awkward moments. Ambassadors normally call on ministers of the receiving government after they present their credentials to the head of state. I decided to seek appointments with the ministers with whose portfolios Australia had most contact, or some semblance of a working relationship. But the only civilian ministers were the Minister for Trade (David Abel, a retired brigadier-general and a Christian who was responsible for ASEAN Free Trade Area issues); the Minister for National Development and National Planning (U Soe Tha, whose responsibilities included coordination of aid, and Australia wasn't giving economic aid to Myanmar at this time); the Minister for Education (U Than Aung), although Australia at that time had stopped offering scholarships to students from Myanmar as part of its sanctions against the military regime; and the Attorney-General (U Tha Tun, who supported human rights development, but died in office in 2002). Even the Minister for Health was a general — Major-General Ket Sein, against whom human rights abuse allegations had been made by human rights activists. (Later, and perhaps more normally, a senior medical doctor was appointed Minister of Health.)

The main ministry that acted as the interface between the diplomatic corps and the military regime was the Ministry of Foreign Affairs. Myanmar has a career foreign service whose personnel were competent and courteous, if not always fully in control of the ministry's policies. Some senior members of the Myanmar foreign service had even been trained in Australia before 1988; the last one being Ambassador Kyaw Tint Shwe, who would become Myanmar Ambassador to the United Nations around 2003. Senior Myanmar diplomats were quite impressive, in particular Deputy Foreign Minister U Khin Maung Win (who was de facto head of the ministry). A few military officers had been transferred to the ministry over the years, to toughen it and to ensure the army knew what ministry staff were thinking. Some, but almost certainly not all, of these officers were known to foreign diplomats. Several became long-term members of the Myanmar foreign service. They did not necessarily perform well, but one exception to this was the long-time Chief of Protocol, Thura Aung Htet, who would recount with feeling his difficult years in the army in the jungle fighting the Burmese Communist Party. On closer acquaintance, by the early 2000s, Myanmar diplomats could be quite frank in private conversations. Sometimes they even went further than might have been expected in official discussion, for example, requesting (publicly available) reports of Asia-Pacific Economic Cooperation (APEC) meetings on a regular basis, even though there was no prospect of Myanmar being invited to join APEC at that time. After the US bombing of Iraq in 2003, one middle-ranking bureaucrat who was in frequent contact with diplomats privately called for similar US action against Myanmar, but such extreme behaviour was rare, and he did not remain long in his job after this.

Given the synergies between the Australian and Myanmar economies, and after consulting Australian NGOs informally, I decided in the first instance to call on the ministers for mines, agriculture, and livestock and fisheries, all of which were sectors of potential direct interest to Australia. Each of these ministers was a general, but each was accustomed to meeting foreign 'dignitaries' in their 'civilian' capacity. The meetings I had with these ministers were vaguely useful, and I recall the Minister of Livestock and Fisheries (Brigadier-General Maung Maung Thein, who was the longest serving minister in the early 2000s) proudly telling me there were no state-owned enterprises under his ministry. The Minister for Agriculture, Major-General Nyunt

Tin, was enthusiastic in supporting agricultural research cooperation with the Australian Centre for International Agricultural Research when this was proposed in 2002, and we signed the government-to-government MOU for the project together.[18] The Minister for Mines, Brigadier-General Ohn Myint, had oversight of the pearl industry, where there was an Australian joint venture.[19] I realised there was a limit to the utility of these calls on other ministers after a particularly unimpressive meeting with the Minister of Industry Number One, (where, by contrast, there were no less than six separate state-owned enterprises). The minister, a retired army officer who was one of the regime's hard-line ideologues, U Aung Thaung, simply rattled off government propaganda and was not in the least interested in engaging with a 'Western' diplomat.[20]

Seeking out civil society: Few alternatives to the military regime

There were few practical alternatives to dealing with the military regime in Myanmar in the early 2000s. One of the frequent observations about Myanmar at that time was that, structurally, civil society weakness was one of the major obstacles to reform and democratic change. This is hardly surprising, given that around two million Burmese, who represented much of the intellectual and financial capital of Myanmar, had left the country after 1988 to live overseas. The non-government sector was indeed unusually weak between 2000–03, having been actively suppressed during Ne Win's one-party rule after 1964. Ne Win had even forced organisations such as the local subsidiary of Rotary International to disband itself, although, by 2003, suggestions for the revival of Rotary in Myanmar

---

18   Major-General Nyunt Tin had been appointed as Minister of Agriculture and Irrigation in 1997, and was dismissed ('permitted to retire') in 2005, supposedly for corruption.

19   This was Myanmar Atlantic Pearl, which was based in Western Australia and operated a pearl farm near Myeik in the far south of Myanmar. See their website: www.myanmarpearl.com/update.htm.

20   According to the editor of *The Irrawaddy* magazine, Aung Thaung was known for his anti-Western views and for his survivor instincts. He later served on the executive of the government's Union Solidarity and Development Association. See Aung Zaw, 'Aung Thaung: Burma's Untouchable Minister', *The Irrawaddy*, Vol. 15, No. 6, June 2007. He stood for election for the USDP in 2010 and was elected, but was not given a ministerial position by President Thein Sein in his new cabinet in March 2011.

began to be heard, but did not gain any headway until more than a decade later. Interestingly, church organisations, including the Young Men's Christian Association (YMCA), continued to function, and several volunteers from Australian counterpart groups were present during this period. The Myanmar Red Cross (MRC) was a government organisation, but the Australian Red Cross considered it a counterpart, and occasionally sent its experts to work at the MRC in Yangon or with ICRC which at that time had numerous offices around the country. The Australian Embassy had good contacts with both the MRC and the ICRC.

After around 1999, it had become possible for local non-governmental organisations to be approved as potential partners for international 'counterparts'. One of the first organisations to be established was an environmental group, the Forest Resource Environment Development and Conservation Association (FREDA), which had been established as early as 1996.[21] Some environmentalists later established another wildlife conservation organisation called the Biodiversity and Nature Conservation Association (BANCA). According to the Ministry of Home Affairs, by 2002 more than 20 local NGOs had been approved,[22] but they were closely watched by the authorities and allowed little freedom of action. Unfortunately, these NGOs were rather fragile and, at that time, did not have a high level of capacity, so there were limited scope for connections between Australia and these groups. (On my return to Australia in 2003, I sought to put BANCA in touch with Birds Australia in the hope that counterpart collaboration could develop.) Historically, there were also a few government-connected humanitarian organisations, such as the Myanmar Anti-Narcotics Association (MANA). Some Australian grass-roots assistance was delivered with the cooperation of local organisations such as the Myanmar YMCA, which was remarkably 'independent', and headed nationally at the time by the respected (Karen Christian) scholar Tun Aung Chain. Such organisations often seemed to have developed pragmatic working relationships with the authorities, who did not interfere unduly with small-scale, local humanitarian initiatives.[23]

---

21 FREDA maintains an impressive website. See: fredamyanmar.com/freda.html.

22 Official communication from the Ministry of Home Affairs to the Australian Embassy.

23 On the other hand, the military regime remained quite suspicious of international agencies and pursued a much more interventionist role in relations to their activities, insisting that programs be coordinated and monitored by the Ministry of National Development and Economic Planning, a policy that was resisted to the extent possible by NGOs and UN agencies.

Embassies that had similar programs (the UK and Japan) had similar experiences, so this was not a unique phenomenon for Australian programs.

Around this time, a few academics and retired bureaucrats with professional qualifications had organised 'academies of science' as a means of keeping in touch with other professionals and fostering future independent professional development. These groups depended to a great extent on retired government officials, but were seriously short of funding. In 2002, the Australian Embassy arranged for a donation of surplus forestry science books from ANU Forestry School (where quite a number of Myanmar foresters had been trained under the Colombo Plan) to be donated to the Academy of Agriculture and Forestry Sciences. These organisations would later proliferate as new vehicles for international cooperation and provide some long-awaited opportunities for strengthening civil society. Also common were some professional associations, a few of which were active, useful, and non-political. The best known was probably the Myanmar Historical Commission, whose regular conference was a major opportunity for interaction between scholars, including, from time to time, some from Australia. There was a further substantial growth in the NGO sector after Cyclone Nargis in 2008, partly as a result of the ongoing need for relief activities for local communities.

Another large and important national Myanmar non-governmental organisation was the Buddhist clergy, or *sangha,* numbering more than 400,000. They were not officially isolated from the outside world, and occasionally travelled overseas. Burma hosted the World Buddhist Summit in December 2004, the year after I left Myanmar, and from around this time began to receive foreigners who wished to undertake meditation courses (a special kind of religious tourism). In the absence of many 'neutral' political observers, I sometimes sought to consult leading independent Buddhists about current affairs. A *sayadaw* I visited on more than one occasion was U Jotika (Zawtika),[24] who was comfortable discussing the current political situation. I met another *sayadaw* who had actually been a political prisoner himself, and who

---

24   U Zawtika (also spelled U Jotika) speaks fluent English, having lived for a short period in the United States. He was living in a small monastery on the outskirts of Bago, about 50 kilometres north of Yangon. Like many prominent *sayadaws* in Myanmar, he has a large popular following for his sermons that he distributes on CDs or tapes. His biodata can be found at www.thisismyanmar.com/nibbana/jotikauk.htm.

was much more nervous about talking (through an interpreter) about such matters. Burmese people quite routinely discuss their daily issues with their *sayadaws*, as we might in a Western society. Some Myanmar *sayadaws* are actively and openly involved in supporting their communities over politically sensitive local issues, but many who were affiliated with the government-controlled *sangha* would not challenge or criticise the military regime.

One sector that was largely 'missing' in Myanmar was the media, both domestic Myanmar media and international media. A trademark of the military regime was its highly effective censorship of the media. Amongst other things, this meant no foreign correspondent was based in Myanmar, apart from the Xinhua representative, and tight controls were exercised over journalistic reporting. But even by 2000, this was starting to change. Foreign media representatives were permitted to enter the country as working journalists from time to time, satellite broadcasting was beginning to have an audience and an impact, and more and more Burmese were tuning into Burmese-language broadcasts by the British Broadcasting Corporation (BBC), Voice of America (VOA), and later (2007) Radio Australia. Although political uses of the media were still in their infancy inside Burma, Aung San Suu Kyi was very effectively using video 'messages' and speeches smuggled out of the country to get her message across directly to international audiences. But even SPDC censorship was being exercised more sensitively in some ways. For example, several international news agencies had long employed highly capable and well-informed local journalists as their 'stringers'. Some of the best media reporting at this interesting transition time was by the stringers for Reuters (Aung Hla Tun) and Associated Press (Aye Aye Win). These two highly professional journalists showed excellent 'instincts' when it came to knowing what developments were important and would be carried by international media. But their reporting was all the more impressive because they succeeded in pushing the boundaries of what reporting the regime would tolerate. Their reports were more accurate, and more timely, and sometimes would have definitely benefited from information provided by military intelligence. Of course, the *Myanmar Times* was operating in a similar way, but it remained constrained by its weekly format and by (initially) appearing only in English.

On one occasion around 2002, I discussed press censorship with the editor-in-chief of one of the main daily Muslim newspapers, who described the form of self-censorship under which he was permitted to operate at that time: his newspaper content was entirely confined to religious matters and not political or social issues. But it seems like the form of 'post-publication censorship' adopted after 2012. At that time, he was not noticeably unhappy about any restrictions on his publishing activities.

5

Myanmar in 2000: Ready Or Not For Change?

In 2000, the Australian Government's assessment of the prospects for movement in Burma seemed about as gloomy as could be imagined.[1] What the assessment did not mention was that the process of political negotiations in Myanmar remained at a complete stalemate, and that the prospects for a resolution of this situation seemed as remote as ever. What it did not need to state was that a repressive, undemocratic military regime was still engaging in widespread human rights abuses and that the leader of the National League for Democracy (NLD), Daw Aung San Suu Kyi, was still under house arrest, with her freedom of movement extremely restricted. Faced at that time with a 'temporary' military regime which had already been in power for more than a decade, and apparently confronting stern outward resistance from the Burmese army military leadership to any overt liberalising openings, it was hard to discern where the inspiration for substantial change

---

1   The entire entry on Burma in the DFAT Annual Report for 1999–2000 read: 'We continued a carefully judged approach to Burma, enabling Mr Downer's Human Rights Institution initiative to proceed to the point where the first human rights training workshops could be held in July, with another one to follow in October 2000. The workshops expose middle-ranking Burmese civil servants to international human rights concepts, instruments and standards. At the same time as implementing this innovative approach, we took care to keep Daw Aung San Suu Kyi and the Burmese opposition fully informed. The department complemented the human rights initiative through direct representations to the Burmese Government about arrests and harassment of members of opposition groups, and other human rights violations. We supported human rights resolutions on Burma at the UN General Assembly and the UN Commission on Human Rights and a resolution on the use of forced labour in Burma at the International Labour Conference.'

could emerge. Yet it was mainly a problem of not knowing enough about the opponents. As the International Crisis Group would comment in its very first report on Myanmar in 2000: 'The challenge for the international community is to find ways — having regard to the regime's apparent strengths and vulnerabilities — to intensify the pressure upon it to accommodate peaceful democratic transition.'[2]

Moreover, as I discovered during my initial exposure to Burmese matters after my appointment was decided upon in early 2000, there were some very slight grounds for hoping that the distasteful military regime in Yangon might be receptive to allowing some change. For example, when Australian Human Rights Commissioner Chris Sidoti visited Myanmar in August 1999, he was surprised by the apparent openness he encountered about exploring the scope for human rights cooperation on the part of regime representatives.[3] At the very least, even a slight hope for positive movement seemed to encourage some international 'players' to contemplate modest initiatives to encourage more movement. Alexander Downer himself was frank about what might or might not be expected from this initiative, when he admitted:

> Now, this one swallow is a long way from making a summer, but the fact that the Burmese Government can see the point of such a (independent human rights) body, albeit not having made up their minds about it, is a good step forward. And it highlights the positive role that Australia can play in advancing discussion of human rights issues throughout our region.[4]

Australia was not alone, however. When I attended a United Nations-sponsored meeting at Walker Hill in Seoul in March 2000 to consider ways forward for Burma, diplomats, experts, and scholars from more than 20 countries were split over whether the best option would involve engagement or further sanctions. At least at this meeting there was debate and discussion on possible ways to move forward.[5] In the

---

2   International Crisis Group, 'Burma/Myanmar: How Strong Is the Military Regime?', Asia Report No. 11, Bangkok and Brussels, 21 December 2000.
3   Sidoti's lengthy and detailed press release can be viewed at www.humanrights.gov.au/news/media-releases/chris-sidoit-visit-myanmar-burma.
4   See Alexander Downer's speech to the NSW Branch of the Australian Institute of International Affairs, 'Australia — Effective Action on Human Rights', 5 August 1999. See foreignminister.gov.au/speeches/1999/990805_aiia.html.
5   See Roger Mitton's report, 'Inside "Secret" Meetings: The Chilston Conferences to Engage Yangon', *Asia Week Online*, March 2000.

previous year (1999), the Burma Update Conference at The Australian National University in Canberra had concluded that 'given the strength of the regime, the relative weakness of the domestic opposition, and the severity of the humanitarian situation, it may be necessary to try to work with the military in order to prepare the ground for the political and economic reform'.[6]

A separate, if related, trend appearing after the mid-1990s was the growing consensus that, notwithstanding the military regime's superficial cohesiveness, there were 'cracks in the edifice' and 'an accommodation with the military regime' probably held the key to making progress towards a political solution of the stand-off between the military regime, its political opponents, and Myanmar society at large.[7] In hindsight, the year 1997 seems to have been a watershed: this was the year the military regime underwent an 'identity change' from State Law and Restoration Council (SLORC) to State Peace and Development Council (SPDC), changing its structure, its personnel and its priorities; it was also the year that Myanmar decided (voluntarily) to coordinate its overall policies more or less to the templates of ASEAN. Whatever shortcomings ASEAN might possess, ASEAN membership was quite a good way to encourage a previously xenophobic and isolationist country to turn its thinking around and to embrace what were for it novel and unprecedented changes.

An important trend throughout Burma's modern history was its strong predilection to seek its own solutions and to make its own choices. One method I used to find out what Myanmar officials might accept was to pose the question: what would be needed for Myanmar to become a 'normal' country after undergoing a process of change which it seemed to be intent on devising for itself, while being conscious of 'lessons' it could learn from other countries? It was encouraging that Myanmar officials did not seem to see their future founded in isolationism or in remaining separate or cut off from the rest of the

---

6   See 'Introduction' to ANU 1999 Burma Update papers: Morten B. Pedersen, Emily Rudland and R. J. May (eds), *Burma Myanmar: Strong Regime Weak State,* Adelaide: Crawford House Publishing, 2000.

7   See the chapters in *Burma Myanmar: Strong Regime Weak State* by Mary Callahan ('Cracks in the Edifice') and Andrew Selth ('The Future of the Burmese Armed Forces'): Morten B. Pedersen, Emily Rudland and R. J. May (eds), *Burma Myanmar: Strong Regime Weak State,* Adelaide: Crawford House Publishing, 2000.

world. Indeed, it was in many ways surprising, but also realistic and reassuring, to find that they might turn to countries such as Australia for assistance and help.

In view of the impenetrability of the Myanmar military and the fragility of the political opposition under police state conditions, it was not surprising that observers looking at Myanmar asked questions about the real potential of non-governmental organisations to act as the harbingers of change in such a tightly controlled state. A few encouraging signs could be found. First, the military regime's gradual acceptance of humanitarian INGOs such as Médecins Sans Frontières, World Vision, and the Cooperative for Assistance and Relief Everywhere (CARE) after 1990. Each of these had a formal MOU with the Myanmar Government. The most significant development in the area of civil society, involving a clear 'back-down' on the part of the regime, was its 1999 agreement to allow the ICRC for the first time ever to visit political prisoners from its office in Yangon, in accordance with standard ICRC procedures. A key role in achieving this outcome for the ICRC was played by the Swiss humanitarian 'field diplomat', Leon de Riedtmatten, who over the next decade was to act as an important mediator in Yangon between the regime and various international agencies, including the ICRC, the United Nations Special Envoys, the International Labour Organization, and the Centre for Humanitarian Dialogue.[8]

The unrecognised potential for civil society to play a larger role was registered by the eminent US scholar David Steinberg at the 1999 Burma Update at The Australian National University in Canberra. While admitting his own pessimism, Steinberg concluded:

> There is no reason why, over time, pluralism and democratic governance may not develop in Burma. The issue for the Burmese is over how long a time; and for foreigners, what role they might play to assist the process.[9]

---

8   De Riedmatten always shuns publicity, and the only description of his role is at th.linkedin. com/pub/leon-riedmatten/48/14b/67a. The regime formally rejected a role for 'mediators', but the enormous contribution of de Riedmatten from 1999 should not be overlooked.

9   See Steinberg's chapter, 'The State, Power and Civil Society in Burma/Myanmar', in Morten B. Pedersen, Emily Rudland and R. J. May (eds), *Burma Myanmar: Strong Regime Weak State,* Adelaide: Crawford House Publishing, 2000.

Analysing the same issue in its second report on Myanmar in 2001, the International Crisis Group (ICG) concluded:

> While civil society organisations will therefore be important in creating the backing for any solution, and in consolidating the democratisation process once it begins, they are not likely to be crucial players in achieving a momentum for change.[10]

The other changes that began around this time were the emergence of business 'cronies' of the military as substantial 'independent' corporate operations. Almost all of Myanmar's modern-day 'crony capitalists' began their corporate development in the early 1990s, deliberately encouraged by the army leadership after 1990. Although demonised by the pro-democracy movement for enjoying unfair benefits from their close associations with the army leadership, crony capitalism was not a new phenomenon in Myanmar.[11] From small beginnings, their reach extended quickly from resources and construction into banking, tourism (hotels, airlines), and other sectors. Eventually, once consolidated as business conglomerates with a wide range of interests after around 2000, many of them would make substantial contributions to infrastructure improvements across the country. The value of their contributions to lifting standards of living and upgrading national physical infrastructure has not been properly acknowledged because of their poor reputations (although, generally, their activities lacked transparency and accountability, and may not have always complied with the provisions of the law). Even at the grass roots, where people in Myanmar were often desperately poor and disadvantaged, they welcomed tourists, their farmers responded quickly to the needs of international markets if they could, and they were interested in the gains from adopting technological change when they could see the advantages of doing so.

The continued opening up of Myanmar after 1988, in direct opposition to the extreme isolationist policies under Ne Win, was a significant change that had wide implications for the possibility of

---

10   International Crisis Group, 'Myanmar: The Role of Civil Society', Asia Report No. 27, Bangkok and Brussels, December 2001.

11   In his 2001 doctoral dissertation, the Myanmar-born political scientist Kyaw Yin Hlaing noted that 'crony capitalism has always thrived [in Burma] and continues to serve as the bedrock of state-business relations throughout the post-colonial period'. Abstract cited at *SOAS Bulletin of Burma Research*, Vol. 2, No. 1 Spring 2004. Available at www.soas.ac.uk/sbbr/editions/file64304.pdf.

political and economic reform as well as potential receptiveness on matters such as human rights, freedom of expression, and freedom of assembly. While this change started with SLORC in 1988, it was hastened by the military regime's 'Visit Myanmar' program in 1996, and was deliberately, but quietly and gradually, extended after 2000. Its political impact was well understood by members of the NLD, one of whom was of the opinion that opening areas of Myanmar for tourism usually resulted in reduced human rights abuses such as forced labour. It was also well understood by religious groups in Western countries such as the United States and Australia, who responded by sending the equivalents of missionaries to provide humanitarian support and educational opportunities for Myanmar people as much as to proselytise. Such groups seemed adept at organising continuous and effective access, even to remote parts of the country such as Chin State and Shan State, and were careful to avoid risky political involvement or gratuitous criticism of the military regime.[12]

In the police state that Myanmar was in the early 2000s, these activities were not only authorised by the Myanmar authorities, they were quietly facilitated and even encouraged. In 2002, I was invited as Australian Ambassador to attend a large graduation ceremony in the Strand Hall, beside the Australian Embassy and alongside the famous Strand Hotel in downtown Yangon, for which the Yangon police provided traffic control. During an officially-approved visit to Kalay in Sagaing State in 2002, I called on the (Burmese) Bishop of Sagaing at his official residence in a large agricultural training centre in the middle of the town. Around this time, I also heard of American trainers carrying out personal management training programs as capacity-building humanitarian activities in the southern part of Myanmar. Such activities were clearly not unusual; they were not held in secret or surreptitiously, but they were conducted discreetly, without publicity, and went without mention in international media. On this basis, they were evidently regarded as not posing political, cultural, or security problems for the authorities or the ordinary Myanmar people they assisted. Indeed, they must have been officially

12   As an example, the American Baptist Church-sponsored Myanmar Institute of Theology in the suburb of Insein in Yangon underwent rapid expansion of its activities from 2000, according to Wikipedia. Its history went back more than 100 years, but, according to its own account, it was permitted to grow substantially and even prosper in the early 2000s. See en.wikipedia.org/wiki/Myanmar_Institute_of_Theology.

regarded as usefully filling gaps when access to quality international education or training was in short supply because of sanctions and Myanmar's 'pariah' status.

In various ways, therefore, by the late 1990s general conditions in Myanmar were better suited to allowing long-awaited political and economic changes to occur. Modest changes at the grass roots level could already be observed at this time, but without any regular and free reporting by local and international media at that time, it was not easy to get information about positive or negative developments, and with all the tools of a police state in full array, it was equally hard to identify what changes were significant and which Myanmar individuals could be expected to deliver 'results'. The prospects were not bright, and the direction, pace, and duration of changes could not be guaranteed or predicted — and, indeed, some would temporarily go into reverse after 2004. Later, after the abolition of the military regime with the change of government, the post-2011 reforms began at a very rapid speed, a development that took many observers by surprise, even though many of the challenges had been recognised, if not addressed, years before.

Another development in the early 2000s was the growth of private international schools around Yangon. It was well known that the Myanmar Government school system was failing and incapable of providing better opportunities that would offer worthwhile employment prospects and greater personal fulfilment. Increasingly, small private schools were being set up, ostensibly to provide English language training or computer skills development, or, in some cases, as preparatory schools to prepare young Burmese for entrance to universities in the US or UK. Some young Australians came to work as 'teachers' in these schools; it was not clear what kind of visas they received or what qualifications they had, but they were not mere short-term visitors. They stayed out of the public eye and apparently managed to avoid causing problems for the ubiquitous Myanmar authorities. The legitimacy of some of these slightly dubious 'international schools' would later be questioned when education reform finally began in Myanmar, but at the time there was no doubt that all of them were tolerated by the authorities, who at this time saw no prospect of Myanmar Government funding for such educational activities. (Myanmar per capita spending on education at this time was appallingly low.)

As ambassador, I was once invited to speak about Australia at one of these American-run 'preparatory schools' in Yangon around this time, a routine invitation which I accepted and which raised no issues for anyone. At this time, there were no Australian Government scholarships available for students from Myanmar, so there was little prospect of Burmese students at such schools going on to study in Australia. However, some enthusiastic, smaller Australian universities were already trying to promote their programs for Burmese private students who might be able to pass entry exams and fund their own studies in Australia, such overseas travel no longer being prohibited for Myanmar citizens. I personally received visits or enquiries from the University of Southern Queensland and Curtin University, both of which seemed enthusiastic about their prospects in Myanmar, but other Australian universities were interested as well. After all, at this stage no Australian Government sanctions against Myanmar would prohibit their campaigns to attract students from Myanmar; only the lack of scholarships or alternative funding would deter Myanmar students from going to Australia.[13]

On the media side, it would be several years before relaxation of Myanmar Government controls over the media occurred, but a surprising number of foreign journalists managed to visit Myanmar during the early 2000s, mostly travelling on tourist visas, obtained quite easily from the Myanmar Embassy in Bangkok. While in Myanmar, such visiting journalists still had to be careful if they were interviewing Burmese nationals, and they often could not travel outside Yangon, but they seemed to be able to go about obtaining material for their reporting without too much trouble, as long as they avoided obvious 'political' topics. Television or film reporting was, however, unusual. I received several requests for interviews from visiting international print journalists — not many of whom were Australians — which I gave at the Australian Embassy in the normal way. Of course, any 'political' comments I made in these interviews were suitably careful, but apart from preferring to be identified only as 'a Western diplomat', I was never aware of any negative consequences from any of these kinds of interviews. I assumed some

---

13   Only later was it revealed that some generals had sent their children to study as private overseas students at Australian universities. I saw this as a positive rather than negative phenomenon, as it implied they were being exposed to Australian values and ideas rather than having closed minds.

other ambassadors in Yangon were doing exactly the same thing — we were not trying to hide any facts about Myanmar from the outside world.

Obviously, the most direct impacts of Myanmar's 'police state' were on its own citizens, not on foreign diplomats, and my anecdotal account is not implying any necessary correlation between what happened to me as a diplomat with the often grim experiences of Myanmar citizens — which they sometimes spoke about. Some retired officials in the early 2000s told how they had been arrested under the Ne Win regime; many claimed this period before 1988 was worse, in terms of ruthless treatment of citizens and arbitrary actions on the part of the authorities, than anything that happened under the SPDC. Of course, in those days few international human rights organisations had access to Myanmar.

One of the main practical problems of dealing with an authoritarian military regime was its inability to be flexible or to negotiate with others. One illustration of this was provide by the relatively affable Minister for Home Affairs, Colonel Tin Hlaing, who in so many ways enjoyed and shone in his role as a de facto politician. In dealing with early instances of extremist Buddhist reactions to Muslims, Tin Hlaing quite often pointed out that, on some of these issues, the authorities had to deal with 'extremists' on both sides, a comment which certainly holds for the debate about Rohingya policies in Myanmar under the Thein Sein Government after 2011.

In 2015, 12 years later after I left Yangon, it is hard to recall just how isolated Myanmar was between 2000–03. Official embassy communications were excellent, following the 1999 worldwide upgrade of the Australian diplomatic communications network, which fortunately included the embassy in Yangon.[14] But other forms of communications with and in Myanmar in 2000 were not so advanced. Landline telephones were subject to interception and frequent breakdowns; mobile phone technology was only just beginning in Myanmar, and relatively few people had access in 2000–03. The internet only began in Myanmar in 2000 (in a highly controlled form),

---

14   Some details of the program to upgrade Australia's diplomatic communications network were contained in the DFAT Annual Report for 1998–99. See dfat.gov.au/about-us/publications/ corporate/annual-reports/annual-report-1998-1999/html/programs/subprog41.htm.

and access was slowly expanding as my assignment concluded in 2003. However, within a couple of years it was possible for me to stay in contact with most Myanmar friends by email. As another example of rapid change, just a few years later I would receive phone calls from friends in Myanmar without this being unusual, for either them or for me.[15] According to the International Telecommunications Union, Myanmar still has one of the lowest per capita rates of access to the internet and mobile telephones, although expansion in both has jumped dramatically since Myanmar's reforms started after 2010.[16]

As an indication of Myanmar's isolation in 2000, perhaps only four international airlines flew direct to Yangon, although the number increased quite quickly after around 2005. The Myanmar postal system was notoriously unreliable and remains so to this day, although registered mail (a requirement of Universal Postal Union membership) usually gets through. Myanmar's middle classes were keen to adopt new information and communications technology (ITC) both professionally and in other ways, but most people in Myanmar initially tended to be quite cautious in how they used these technologies. Moreover, the potential connection between modern telecommunications technology and political liberalisation was predictably of considerable concern on the part of the Myanmar military regime, who often used technical breaches of ITC laws for internal security purposes.[17] All forms of communication technology — facsimiles, internet-connected computers, mobile phones — could be targeted by the authorities for potential political abuses.

Under the military regime, satellite television access was notionally more tightly controlled at the personal level than other forms of ITC, but this did not seem to stop satellite dishes appearing around the country after 2000. In 2000–03 international free-to-air satellite broadcasting was already spreading rapidly, and was uncensored, so some footage of the 9/11 incident in New York was instantly available, FA Cup football

---

15   Myanmar's standing in international data on the diffusion on new telecommunications technology was always poor, but my own experience has been that generally those who wanted access could get it.

16   See ITU statistics on telecommunications diffusion at www.itu.int/en/ITU-D/Statistics/Pages/stat/default.aspx.

17   One of the first steps taken by the National League for Democracy after 2011 was to establish its own website, which made a visible difference to its profile, even if the website was not fully developed. Later it was closed down and replaced.

matches were routinely screened at local pubs and 'tea houses', and major international events were seen in one form or another. Within a few years, satellite dishes could be seen in cities and even in small and remote towns all over the country, showing the keen desire of the ordinary people to enjoy access to at least some of what the rest of the world could see. By 2005, Democratic Voice of Burma started television broadcasts directly to Myanmar, and these broadcasts influenced the unfolding of the 'Saffron Revolution' in 2007.

In a relatively minor way, in 2000–03 Australia was inevitably involved in some of these advances in new ITC in Myanmar. The Australian Broadcasting Corporation's Radio Australia had long collected evidence of its loyal short-wave radio listenership in Myanmar; and when Australia Television International (ATVI) was launched in 2002,[18] it also found an audience in Myanmar, even though its signal did not target Myanmar and was not strong there. Australian missions in Southeast Asia, including the Australian Embassy in Yangon, were asked at this time to assist ATVI in getting started with local audiences.[19] Myanmar's isolation was somewhat mitigated by the subsequent arrival of ATVI at some of Yangon's hotels in early 2003. Although Myanmar was at the western edge of the satellite footprint, it could be received there and, following an exploratory visit to Yangon by ATVI representatives, after it was installed in a few hotels in Yangon in early 2003, it was instantly popular, reflecting the general appetite for such things in Myanmar. (Myanmar was not even an official target country and there would not have been many paid-up subscribers.)

---

18 See Alexander Downer's speech on the occasion of the launch, entitled 'Australia, the Asia–Pacific, and Television: Broadcasting to the Region', 13 February 2002, at www.foreignminister.gov.au/speeches/2002/020213_fa_austv_launch.html.

19 As the DFAT Annual Report for 2002–03 blandly said: 'The department and posts worked closely with ABCAP (ABC Asia Pacific) TV to secure entry into regional markets.' In 2002, the ABC launched ABC Asia Pacific or ABCAP — the replacement for the defunct Australia Television International (ATVI) operated previously by the Seven Television Network.

6
Engagement Versus Disengagement

At the time of my appointment as Ambassador to Burma/Myanmar, there was an ongoing debate over 'engagement versus disengagement', which would run through the early 2000s. Earlier initiatives seeking to engage with the Myanmar military regime, such as the 'benchmarks' proposals of Alexander Downer's predecessor as foreign minister, Gareth Evans, had failed conspicuously to win support from either the international community or the military regime. These 'benchmarks', floated as early as 1992, suffered from being more dirigiste, more prescriptive, more rigorous, and more redolent of international pressure than other 'openings'.[1] Not much of this debate about engagement versus disengagement surfaced in public in Australia, but it was very much to the forefront in government-to-government diplomatic contacts at the time: it would routinely arise in Australia's participation in expanded ASEAN meetings, and with Australia's 'like-minded' regional partners, such as Japan.[2]

---

1   Gareth Evans reflected publicly on this failure for the first time when opening The Australian National University's Myanmar Update on 5 June 2015. See his remarks at www.gevans.org/speeches/speech573.html. Even his efforts to visit Myanmar as foreign minister up until 1996, or as President of the International Crisis Group from 2000–09, were rebuffed by the military regime at the time. He was not to visit Myanmar in this kind of role until 2014.

2   Alexander Downer mentioned the broader context of his initiative with Burma in an address to the NSW Branch of the Australian Institute of International Affairs on 5 August 1999, referring to 'the benefit of concentrating on outcomes rather than rhetoric in bilateral human rights diplomacy'. See foreignminister.gov.au/speeches/1999/990805_aiia.html.

One motivation for closer engagement with the military regime at this time was the possibility that it might be susceptible to being persuaded to introduce political change. This was not necessarily an unrealistic expectation: for a variety of reasons, the post-1988 military regime had chosen to drop Ne Win's policy of isolation and to open up Myanmar (to foreign investment, tourism, etc.); while the regime was secretive and suspicious, and while it often denied many international observers access, it was also allowing much more exposure and scrutiny of the country through UN agencies and its participation in ASEAN than previous Burmese governments. Moreover, Myanmar remained a member of most UN agencies and international financial institutions, although its participation was not necessarily very active.

Obviously, the countries with potentially the greatest influence, or leverage, were the major powers who could, hypothetically or otherwise, offer the most aid, or business and investment. Australia was not in this league. By the end of the twentieth century, US policymakers had come up with new foreign policy instruments which the United States could apply unilaterally, either under presidential authority or certification, or congressional processes — for example, legislation with built-in accountability mechanisms. Often these involved the categorisation of countries as compliers or non-compliers with international conventions or with unilateral US requirements where US policymakers did not regard international conventions as sufficient. Frequently, this would involve the US Government compiling a 'black list' of countries deemed to be at fault, who would not qualify to receive any beneficial treatment from the US Government. The only way to qualify for US assistance, for a country on such a list, would be for the president to 'de-certify' the country in question, usually on the request or recommendation of the US Congress. Narcotics, human rights, and weapons proliferation were the most common subjects of these lists. 'Burma' was very often on these lists. Australia had no capacity to apply such policies, even though sometimes they matched Australian policy objectives. At times, US officials tried to use these procedures to shift the behaviour of non-complying countries such as Myanmar, but at other times it served US interests to be able to 'name and shame' certain countries by publicising their non-conformity.

Sometimes US policy was painted into a corner by the ideological imperatives close to the heart of many members of the US Congress, to which US administrations needed to be extremely sensitive. Among these reporting mechanisms were the annual reports on religious freedoms, which presented a highly critical image of Myanmar. To people on the ground in Myanmar, this criticism seemed remote from what one saw around the streets of multicultural Yangon, with its numerous cathedrals, mosques, and Buddhist temples and shrines; a panoply of religious events with designated official holidays for every major religion; mass Christian events in the form of festivals or theological college degree awards ceremonies; the substantial Catholic/Protestant enclaves which one saw when visiting the middle of cities such Yangon (in Insein), or Kalay (in Sagaing State); and in the form of charitable activities or organisations such as the YMCA. Few authoritarian states have a Ministry of Religious Affairs, but Myanmar/Burma has always had such a ministry, reflecting the importance Buddhism plays in society. It was not inappropriate that, under the military regime, the Minister for Religious Affairs was usually a general (since the military were quite comfortable being both Buddhists and soldiers).

Essentially, the usual methods for influencing other countries were either through some form of active engagement *with* the government, or through the imposition of costs and punishment *against* the government via sanctions. In other words, 'carrots and sticks'. Australian policy towards Myanmar after 1988 followed a little of both approaches. Australia clearly aligned itself with criticism of Burma's anti-democratic regime and widespread human rights abuses, but, privately, Australia sought to differentiate itself from the countries pursuing hard-line unilateral sanctions by not ruling out certain kinds of direct engagement with the military regime. Australia was among a small group of Western countries that still provided humanitarian assistance, mainly through UN agencies and NGOs.

US sanctions against Myanmar were, unsurprisingly, a major source of irritation as far as the Myanmar Government was concerned. Myanmar officials — and the Myanmar official media — missed no opportunity to criticise US sanctions as being unfair, discriminatory, involving double standards, and punitive in their impact on the ordinary Myanmar people and the Myanmar economy — which Myanmar officials did not attempt to deny. In 2003, the official Burmese media even publicised a petition from the Myanmar business community to the US Government protesting against the loss of jobs as a result of US bans on garment imports from Myanmar. Unsurprisingly, the Myanmar Government steadfastly denied that US sanctions had any political impact, either in terms of attracting wider international support or in the sense of influencing the State Peace and Development Council (SPDC) to change policies. In a later chapter, I examine the evidence that certain US sanctions had quite a powerful and direct economic impact.

One focus of the 'engagement versus disengagement' debate that affected ordinary people — in Myanmar and elsewhere — was tourism. Even in 2000, the Lonely Planet guide to Myanmar (Burma) (already in its seventh edition)[3] still felt the need to begin with an introduction in which it sought to defend its promotion of tourism to Myanmar by answering the question: 'Should you visit Myanmar?' Its publishers, Australians Tony and Maureen Wheeler, lived in Melbourne and visited Myanmar from time to time — including while I was there — to keep in touch with developments, and to ensure the integrity of the Lonely Planet's research on Myanmar. Their introduction sets out the different nuances between Aung San Suu Kyi/National League for Democracy (NLD) and government-in-exile (NCGUB) views about tourism: the expatriate views tended to be harder, arguing that 'much' of any tourism revenue 'went into the pockets of the ... generals'.[4] The Wheelers obviously favoured tourists visiting Myanmar, but were openly unsympathetic to the military regime and were, unsurprisingly, very dismissive of the military regime's 1997 'Visit Myanmar' campaign.

Pressure for sanctions against Burma was mobilised through 'Burma Campaigns', broadly supported by the NLD, which resulted in the European Union adopting a 'Common Position' on Burma in 1996, discouraging trade and investment, and calling for a tourism boycott. However, many EU member governments did no more than urge companies to apply boycotts, without imposing any enforcement —

---

3   The first Lonely Planet guide to Burma appeared in 1979. It was not unusual when travelling around Myanmar even much later to meet tourism sector workers claiming proudly to have assisted the Wheelers undertake their research.
4   Some of the arguments for and against the boycott are outlined in Andrew Buncombe, 'Boycott Burma: To go or not to go?', Independent, 2 June 2008. Available at www.independent. co.uk/travel/news-and-advice/boycott-burma-to-go-or-not-to-go-837207.html.

although the absence of legal sanctions against tourism was not always made clear to the public. European tourism was indeed discouraged, but it continued at a low level. Responding to different pressures, Australian governments openly proclaimed their unwillingness to contemplate restrictions on trade, investment, and tourism, but did not promote any of these activities officially; they were never tempted to associate themselves with economic sanctions until 2007, when the 'Saffron Revolution' occurred amidst international publicity.

During this period, Australia was seen by all concerned as belonging to the engagement camp, even though it had not eased its political sanctions and did not deviate from its basic association with Western policies against the military regime. So it would be more accurate to characterise Australian policies at this time as directed towards 'limited engagement'. Myanmar was a country of limited direct significance for Australia, and Australian policies were reasonably altruistic, motivated by what was best for the people, the country, and the region. This was not always the case, but with Burma/Myanmar the 'historical baggage' for Australia was smaller than usual. Australia was widely regarded internationally as being well intentioned in relation to Myanmar. If Australia's approach was at times a little more independent, this seemed to be expected by the international community and was respected by most of the people of Myanmar. The only Myanmar organisation that openly sought different Australian policies was the NLD, which favoured sanctions and wanted all Western countries to follow a single-minded approach. (The NLD also at times criticised Japan for diverging from the mainstream Western approach.)

When he was Australian Foreign Minister (1987–96), Gareth Evans perhaps straddled this engagement versus sanctions approach, articulating what he called his 'benchmarks' for actions by Myanmar a proposal he launched officially via the ASEAN-Plus meetings around 1995. In his opening address at the 2015 Myanmar Update Conference at The Australian National University in June 2015, he reflected ruefully on the lack of support he had received domestically and internationally for his proposals.[5] Perhaps these ideas were ahead of the times. But they were also probably far more prescriptive than a 'sovereignty sensitive' regime could tolerate.

---

5   See gevans.org/speeches/speech573.html.

While Western governments maintained their official sanctions on political contacts with the SPDC into the first decade of the twenty-first century, and while restrictions on multilateral, including UN, 'engagement' remained, some other countries — including Myanmar's Asian neighbours — gradually relaxed their attitude towards the SPDC in the late 1990s. Moreover, following the SPDC's more cooperative attitude and the release of Aung San Suu Kyi from de facto house arrest in May 2002, a few other 'Western' governments experimented by reinstating ministerial visits. Most significant were the visits in August 2002 by the Japanese and Australian foreign ministers after gaps of 19 years in both cases. Regrettably, the more moderate SPDC policies did not last beyond May 2003, when regime-sponsored thugs attacked Aung San Suu Kyi and regime policy hardened again, to be met with new Western sanctions.

It is difficult to say whether the division in Western policies towards Myanmar in this period generated problems, or whether it served useful political and/or economic purposes, either in creating leverage with Myanmar or differentiating Australian policy from that of other countries. It certainly had a slightly polarising effect, in that Australia and Japan (and to a certain extent Korea) were openly recognised as pursuing policies distinct from the US and the UK. The SPDC definitely realised this, but did not try to take unreasonable advantage of it. Ordinary educated Myanmar citizens were quite aware of these distinctions between different Western countries, and did not seem to find them confusing or complicating. Interestingly, but perhaps unsurprisingly, international agencies (including UN agencies) seemed to quite strongly welcome the more accommodating policies of Australia and Japan, in preference to the hard-line attitudes of the US and the UK that, in the end, had the very real effect of denying substantial funding to international agencies. Thus UN Secretary-General's Special Envoy Razali Ismail was delighted to attend one of the Australia Government's human rights workshops, which coincided with one of his visits, and UN Special Rapporteur on Human Rights Paulo Sérgio Pinheiro was later prepared to praise the workshops in one of his reports. (Both the US and UK governments officially complained about these workshops when they started.) Agencies such as UNHCR and UNICEF were explicit in expressing privately their appreciation for Australian support for their activities in Myanmar. When the ILO was seeking a special envoy to rescue their cooperation program on forced labour, it was no accident that they found the ideal candidate in former Australian Governor-General Sir Ninian Stephen, who was to visit Myanmar in 2001 and 2005.[6] So Australia's rhetoric was sometimes matched with action, and Australia's reputation for independence in its policy thinking sometimes paid dividends.

The constant absence of high-level US policy involvement with Myanmar was a key reason for the failure of US policy. Political contact between the United States and Myanmar had been kept at a very low level ever since 1988, even when Aung San Suu Kyi was released from house arrest in May 2002. Visits in either direction by members of the cabinets of either country remained prohibited under US sanctions. Visits to Rangoon by members of the US Congress were few and far between, and even the number of congressional staffers who visited was extremely small. The possibility of a visit by the then Assistant Secretary of State for East Asian and Pacific Affairs, James Kelly, was discussed during 2002–03, but never materialised before Aung San Suu Kyi was again placed under detention. Visits by the relevant Deputy Assistant Secretary of State for East Asian and Pacific Affairs occurred from time to time, but were predominantly of a fact-finding and familiarisation nature, rather than offering the possibility of a substantial political dialogue, let alone any prospect of a change in US policy. In the absence of any inter-governmental programs between the United States and Myanmar, the only other US officials who visited were those working on counter-narcotics policy and, later and only intermittently, on the recovery of World War II remains. There would be few (non-communist) countries in the world where the United States so systematically avoided high-level political exchanges.

A further complication was the fact that since 1991 the head of the US Embassy was designated chargé d'affaires rather than ambassador, as part of the US Congress's political sanctions against Myanmar. In practical terms, this did not normally make a great deal of difference in Yangon. The US Chargé d'Affaires was usually active in cultivating influential members of the Myanmar community, enjoyed frequent

---

6   See International Labour Office, 'Developments Concerning the Question of the Observance by the Government of Myanmar of the Forced Labour Convention: Report of High Level Team', Geneva, November 2001. Available at www.ilo.org/public/english/standards/relm/gb/docs/gb282/pdf/gb-4-ax.pdf.

access to Aung San Suu Kyi, the NLD and other opposition groups, and in a highly pragmatic way developed discreet but effective ties in conjunction with the Myanmar military through the military attachés stationed in the US Embassy.

But the absence of an 'ambassador' inevitably constrained working relations and inhibited the development of meaningful substantive rapport between Washington and Yangon. For example, the US Embassy had more limited contacts within the Myanmar bureaucracy than would normally have been the case for the United States, even though the bureaucracy is essentially technocratic. Instead, the embassy concentrated its outreach to opposition organisations and individuals whose political influence in the tightly controlled environment of Myanmar was not necessarily very significant.[7] Staff of the US Embassy were reportedly monitored more closely by the Myanmar security authorities than the staff of most other embassies, and could not normally travel as freely (although US Embassy officers were able to visit the site of the 30 May 2003 Depayin attack on the NLD convoy, despite the lack of any official travel permit).[8] It is probably the case that the absence of ambassador-level representation had greater negative impact in Washington, where a chargé d'affaires, appointed by the State Department rather than the White House, simply would not have the same influence in Congress or the White House when it came to getting the ear of high-level policymakers in Washington.

Even though Congress blocked the appointment of an ambassador after 1990 — and continued to do so until 2012 — and refused approval for any government-to-government assistance programs, the US Defense Department normally maintained three defence attachés in the US Embassy, while the Central Intelligence Agency maintained a

---

7   Unsurprisingly perhaps, one did not hear, even anecdotally, about participants in these programs appearing in more prominent roles. A much later US study revealed some movement of these 'alumni' into influential positions in the Myanmar Government, but not in the numbers or at the level that might have been expected. See Mark S. Riley and Ravi A. Balaram, 'The United States International Military Education and Training (IMET) Program with Burma/Myanmar: A Review of the 1980–1988 Programming and Prospects for the Future', *Asian Affairs: An American Review*, Vol. 40, No. 3, pp. 109–132.

8   The State Department occasionally made public mention of this harassment, but in a relatively mild way. An example is the State Department's October 2003 'Report on Activities to Support Democracy Activities in Burma as Required by the Burmese Democracy and Freedom Act of 2003'.

presence and discreet, but limited, working relations with Myanmar counterparts. US contacts with the *Tatmadaw* (Burmese armed forces) at times were quite good, mainly through 'golf course diplomacy', but of course this could not be followed up with the usual military cooperation and training programs. The last members of the *Tatmadaw* to receive training in the United States were those who had been sent there in the last years of the Ne Win regime, before 1990. Few of these last members of Burmese military to receive training in the United States were in positions of influence by 2000.[9] As a result, the network of American alumni in the Burmese army dwindled, as it did in other circles in Myanmar. The same thing happened with most other Western aid donor countries' networks. It could probably be said that the United States does not necessarily recoil from working with a military government in another country, as do many other Western countries.

By 2000, the central focus of US policies towards 'Burma' was the various economic sanctions imposed unilaterally under US legislation, some of them at the instigation of the US Congress against the wishes of the administration of the day. After the 1988 uprising, the United States was the leading proponent of economic sanctions, beginning with the ban on new investment from 1997, but Western allies of the United States adopted similar sanctions, especially after the 'Saffron Revolution' of 2007. However, the United States also imposed a range of political and security measures administratively, and these were generally followed by other OECD member countries, including Australia. US diplomats were clearly glad that a group of like-minded countries had taken a strong stance against the 1988 military takeover in Burma, but they did not insist that all Western countries follow them in adopting economic sanctions. Indeed, they seemed to think that to have some diversity in policies provided additional flexibility in dealing with the military regime. They were always interested in how Australia's 'limited engagement' approach was faring. Aung San Suu Kyi tended to be sceptical about limited engagement and sometimes expressed her regret that Australian policies were not more like those of the US.

9   In 2013, when their review of the program with Myanmar was published, Riley and Balaram found only four persons serving at ministerial level or above.

Of course, the United States sometimes pursued its own form of engagement with Myanmar's military regime. One area where this was in evidence was the counter-narcotics programs. Some US Drug Enforcement Agency officers were assigned to the US Embassy and worked quite closely with the relevant areas of the Myanmar Police Force, as well as providing technical and other assistance through the then United Nations Drug Cooperation Program (UNDCP). The Australian Federal Police pursued a very similar approach, and cooperated closely with the Myanmar Police Force in Yangon. US pressure on Myanmar to be more vigorous in suppressing opium production was strong, and included a failed attempt in 2003 to arrange for leading Myanmar Central Committee for Drug Abuse Control representatives to give briefings for the relevant Congressional committees in the hope that this would allow Myanmar to be certified as a cooperating country. The briefings happened, but the certification did not, leaving Myanmar Police leadership very embarrassed and quite mistrustful of US promises. That was the last time prior to 2009 that the US Government pursued any kind of engagement.

After 2003, US policy towards Myanmar moved away from engagement, hardening just as the military regime's policies hardened. Additional US economic sanctions were imposed after the detention of Aung San Suu Kyi following the Depayin incident, and again after the regime crushed the unarmed and peaceful 'Saffron Revolution'. US rhetoric and public posture towards Myanmar also hardened. Myanmar was not included in George W. Bush's 2002 'Axis of Evil' inauguration speech, but it was among the 'Outposts of Tyranny' described by incoming Secretary of State Condaleeza Rice in 2005. Both President Bush and his wife associated much more actively with Burmese democracy activists. Lobbying from US think tanks such as the National Bureau of Research, the Asia Society, and the US Institute of Peace that called for more flexible policies was ignored, until Hillary Clinton — on assuming the position of Secretary of State in the Obama Administration in 2009 — announced that 'all US policies towards Myanmar had failed', and called for a new policy strategy.

For its part, the Myanmar Government was relatively pragmatic in its dealings with US representatives. It granted high-level access to the US Chargé d'Affaires,[10] and only rarely excluded the US Chargé d'Affaires from activities for ambassadors. Its own ambassador in Washington was always a very senior diplomat who was trusted to carry out an active campaign of defensive lobbying on behalf of the SPDC, and who managed remarkably well in the intensive and demanding political environment of Washington. The US Chargé d'Affaires, Priscilla Clapp, was granted immediate access to Secretary One of the SPDC, General Khin Nyunt, after the terrorist attacks on the Twin Towers in New York on 11 September 2001, and the Myanmar Vice Foreign Minister, U Khin Maung Win, signed the condolence book opened by the US Embassy after the incident. The SPDC was extremely cooperative in meeting US requests for extra security thereafter. Even a mid-level US official, such as Deputy Assistant Secretary of State for East Asian and Pacific Affairs Matthew Daley, was granted meetings with Khin Nyunt in May 2002.

The verdict on the merits and demerits of US sanctions is by no means clear. While, judging from their voting record, few politicians in the US Congress seemed to have had reservations about US sanctions, more rigorous analysis tends to cast serious doubt on the overall impact of economic sanctions in particular. A number of academics have condemned US sanctions for being ineffective, counter-productive, and impairing US policy options more than they impaired the SPDC's freedom of manoeuvre.[11] Generally, they have called for a more sophisticated policy approach, incorporating some form of engagement.

Political relations between the EU — especially the UK — and Myanmar had been deliberately limited after the EU adopted its 'Common Position' on Myanmar in 1996. When EU sanctions were extended to an arms embargo and assets freeze in April 2000, the

---

10   But the Myanmar Ambassador in Washington was always subject to the travel restrictions that Western countries imposed in reciprocity for the restrictions imposed on all diplomats in Myanmar.

11   See, for example: David Steinberg, 'The United States and Its Allies: The Problem of Burma/ Myanmar Policy', *Contemporary Southeast Asia*, Vol. 29, No. 2, August 2007, pp. 219–237; Ian Holliday, 'Rethinking the United States's Myanmar Policy', *Asian Survey*, Vol. 45, No. 4, July/ August 2005, pp. 603–621; and Mike and Gail Billington, 'US, Not Myanmar is Isolating Itself', *Economist Intelligence Report*, 30 July 2004.

way was also opened for an EU 'Troika' (made up of representatives of the Foreign Ministry of the Presidency of the Council of the European Union, the European Commissioner for External Relations, and the Common Foreign and Security Policy Secretariat) to engage in political 'dialogue'. The Troika initiative with Burma never really worked during 2000–03: their visits were often postponed and, when they did come, they often did not meet the highest level Myanmar representatives, and they had no decision-making mandate. Perhaps because they were senior officials rather than political representatives, and because EU policy seemed fairly fixed and it was not clear that the Troika could devise a different policy, the Troika did not seem to be taken seriously by the Myanmar Government. EU engagement was not to start in earnest until the EU began offering substantial aid after 2006. Subsequently, the Troika idea was quietly sidelined by EU policymakers.

In this period, Japan sometimes seemed to be in two minds about 'sanctions versus engagement'. Japan's structural adjustment initiative from 2000–01 was ambitious in endeavouring to use a process of engagement, in the form of a highly structured dialogue, to be the catalyst for policy change across several sectors of the economy. The dialogue was between Japanese officials and private economists, and relevant senior Myanmar Government representatives led by the minister attached to the Prime Minister's Office, Brigadier-General David Abel. The choice of Abel as the leader of the Myanmar representatives was no accident: he had the most experience in international affairs of any SPDC minister, was well informed about economic policy, and was known to favour reform. Others among the Myanmar representatives — equally carefully chosen — were key policymakers in the main economic agencies and the central bank. In launching the initiative, the Japanese Government had the full support of the Japanese business community, and enlisted the cooperation of the relevant Japanese semi-government aid agencies, as well as certain Japanese academics. These Japanese academics were quite familiar with Myanmar through their participation in earlier Japanese Government-funded projects providing 'intellectual' support and 'policy input'. Thus some of the Japanese academics were also well known to the Myanmar participants, which would have been important in contributing to the goal of trust building between the two sides. While the program apparently did not attract public criticism in Japan — being given minimal publicity by the Japanese Government — it probably would not have enjoyed the wholehearted support of the ruling Liberal Democratic Party, which was split between those politicians who supported providing assistance to the SPDC and those who did not.

The initiative was carried forward through a series of workshops focused on policies for reforming the Myanmar economy, which covered four fields: fiscal and monetary policy; trade and industrial policy; information technology; and agriculture and rural development.[12] These workshops were held, without publicity, alternately in Tokyo and Yangon, again emphasising the 'equivalence' of the two sides. Japanese participants in the project tended to be enthusiastic about the opportunity it provided to discuss various policy options in a closed environment. The project provided an opportunity to openly canvas policy choices that it would not have otherwise been possible to raise, let alone debate. Lively discussions occurred, especially about strengthening market forces on agriculture and exports, and financial and monetary policy. At a time when the Myanmar Government was giving new emphasis to agribusiness and agricultural exports, some of the subjects of the workshop seemed extremely relevant. Myanmar participants certainly hoped that this initiative might encourage the SPDC leadership to accept the need for policy changes in areas such as the exchange rate and agriculture. Expectations that the project might lead to substantial Japanese assistance were never completely dismissed.[13]

Eventually, joint reports containing 'agreed' policy recommendations were prepared in each area. Considerable discussion took place before these conclusions were finalised, with quite sensitive issues being openly broached. Draft conclusions for the report on sensitive areas were cleared with the highest levels of the SPDC before being incorporated into the reports. This often meant a watering down of the recommendations. It was hoped by all concerned that the recommendations, once finally agreed for the reports, would go to the Myanmar Government and be adopted. Japan's expectations in this regard were to be disappointed. The joint reports remain confidential

---

12   The only Japanese Government statement about the initiative on the public record is a Ministry of Foreign Affairs press release, dated 21 November 2001, entitled 'Yangon Workshop on Japan–Myanmar Cooperation for Structural Adjustment in the Myanmar Economy'. Referring to the third of four workshops, the press release contains only the barest of information.
13   Author's private conversations with Myanmar and Japanese participants, Yangon 2002.

and their content has never been publicly revealed, although third country experts who were shown copies in confidence confirm that they contained substantive and well-focused policy solutions.[14]

The program achieved some significant progress in enabling unprecedented frank discussions on sensitive policy issues, and the consideration of results and impacts from implementing the policy reforms. However, the program failed in its ultimate goal of obtaining SPDC commitment to introduce economic reforms. Despite the offer of quite specific incentives (the promise of a sizeable Japanese Government loan to cushion the impact of structural changes following a rationalisation of the exchange rates), this was too strong a medicine for the conservative and essentially non-reforming military regime. The Japanese Government's final report was somewhat delayed in being presented for decision and, by the time it was considered, the military leadership was no longer receptive to the idea of changing economic policy. Brigadier-General David Abel was eventually dropped from his ministerial position in late 2003, the last minister with any true understanding of economic policy.[15]

---

14   Information received from third-country academic, September 2005.
15   The only informed article published on this program is 'Myanmar de Mieta Chiteki Enjo no Igi to Kadai' ('The Significance of and Issues Experienced in Intellectual Assistance in Myanmar') by Ryu Fukui, Deputy Head, International Cooperation Department, Japan Development Bank, which appeared in the 'Towareru Nihon no Kokusai Kyoryoku' ('Debating Japan's International Cooperation') column in *Kokusai Kaihatsu Janaru* [*International Development Journal*], July 2003, p. 13. Fukui was one of the Japanese experts who participated in the project. Little else is written on the project because of the confidentiality agreement entered into by the Japanese Government in order to launch the program.

Australian Ambassador's residence and garden, Yangon (2002)

Source: Author's collection

Australian Club buildings taken from Ambassadors' residence (2002)

Source: Author's collection

At opening of the refurbished Australian Embassy,
Strand Road (2000)
Source: Myanmar Times

Signing MOU on HIV AIDS cooperation with Myanmar Police
Force (2002)
Source: Olivia Cable, Museum in Commemoration of Opium-Free in Special Region 4

Thanbyuzayat Commonwealth War Cemetery – Entrance gate and gravestones
Source: Author's collection

Thanbyuzayat War Cemetery gravestones (2002)
Source: Author's collection

Map of Burma-Thailand Railway
Source: The Australian National University CartoGIS

At an Australia Day Reception at the Australian Club,
Yangon (2003)

Aung San Suu Kyi in crowd after her release (2002) (Mandalay)
Source: Mizzima News

Christine Wilson meeting Aung San Suu Kyi 10 years later
at The Australian National University
Source: The Australian National University

7

Australia's 'Limited Engagement' Initiatives

Engagement was seen — somewhat controversially at the time — as a means by which Australia might influence a receptive Myanmar Government, albeit it a military regime internationally held in ill repute. What was most significant was that Australian assistance initiatives were to be carried out on a government-to-government basis. Australian Foreign Minister Alexander Downer had first set out his policy of 'engagement' with Burma on human rights in an article in the *International Herald Tribune* on 23 August 1999.[1] In a very persuasive way, he said:

> Australia believes that now is the time to engage the regime in a serious dialogue on the protection and promotion of human rights in Burma. Such a dialogue is one way of improving the lot of ordinary Burmese. It is also a means of drawing the regime into a discussion on issues that have caused great concern outside Burma. To do nothing is to fail to confront the problem.

Alexander Downer had come up with the idea of enlisting the support of Australia's then Human Rights Commissioner Chris Sidoti to develop a program of human rights capacity building, to prepare the way for the eventual establishment of a national human rights institution

---

1   Alexander Downer, 'A Start to Help Set Burmese on the Road to Human Rights', *International Herald Tribune*, 23 August 1999.

complying with international norms, something that was at that time unthinkable for an international community strongly committed to sanctions against the pariah military regime.

Foreign Minister Downer responded to Myanmar's membership of ASEAN and met his counterpart, SLORC Foreign Minister Ohn Gyaw, on 26 July 1997 at the first ASEAN Regional Forum attended by Myanmar. Downer continued to meet Ohn Gyaw — and his successor U Win Aung — at these meetings from time to time. In order to explore the parameters of possible cooperation between Australia and Myanmar in the area of human rights, Chris Sidoti visited Myanmar in August 1999. According to the media release issued in Sidoti's name: 'The principal purpose of the visit was to discuss with officials of the Government of Myanmar the nature, roles and functions of independent national human rights institutions established in accordance with the relevant international standards, the "Paris Principles".'[2] According to Sidoti, in his preliminary discussion with Home Affairs Minister Tin Hlaing, and subsequently with SPDC Secretary One Lieutenant-General Khin Nyunt, the Myanmar leadership indicated that it understood exactly the significance of this initiative and its ground-breaking nature, both for the military regime and for the international community. They went into the program fully conscious of the undertakings they were entering into, and of the desirability of bringing around Aung San Suu Kyi.[3] Eventually, it was agreed that this might be achieved by conducting a series of workshops for Myanmar Government bureaucrats and law enforcement officials. This decision was strongly criticised by the Australian Labor Party, supporters of the Burmese democracy movement in Australia, and (in private) by some foreign governments — but not by United Nations representatives, who strongly backed the initiative and took opportunities to demonstrate their support through public statements and by observing some of the workshops.[4]

---

2   Sidoti summarised the outcomes of his visit in a media release, in which he noted 'that an exchange of views on human rights has begun where none existed before; that we have been able to identify some areas in which cooperation may be possible; and that there is evidently a strong commitment to taking the process further.' The media release issued on 5 August 1999 can be accessed at www.humanrights.gov.au/.

3   Personal interview with Chris Sidoti, 18 November 2014.

4   On 28 June 2000, the then ALP Shadow Foreign Minister Laurie Brereton called for the program to be cancelled. See www.burmalibrary.org/reg.burma/archives/200007/msg00015.html.

Alexander Downer had occasion to vigorously defend his initiative in August 2000, saying:

> Our approach to Burma arose from the repeated failure of other approaches to improve the political and human rights situation there. The Human Rights training program has not only helped educate Burmese officials in basic human rights, but we have also contributed to Burma agreeing to establish an independent Human Rights Commission based on the Paris Principles, and using Indonesia's KOMNAS HAM as a model. These are the only positive developments in human rights in Burma over the past decade.[5]

By 2001, Alexander Downer went as far as saying he detected 'signs of movement' in the democratic process: 'We take the view that some sort of engagement with them is better than none. We have been trying to explore ways we can engage without engaging too warmly.'[6] Myanmar Government representatives were sounded out on whether they were interested in modest engagement initiatives directly targeting areas for reform. When they responded positively, as they generally did, this certainly opened the way for significant communication space with different arms of the Myanmar Government. Sidoti confirms that the SPDC fulfilled all the undertakings they made to him as Alexander Downer's representative.

Trust building through the Ministry of Home Affairs

The Australian Government's cooperation on human rights training with the Ministry of Home Affairs was certainly an example of trying to build trust through a responsive government agency and its leading individuals. The then Minister for Home Affairs, retired Colonel Tin Hlaing, was a close associate of Lieutenant-General Khin Nyunt, was one of the longer serving military ministers, and as the minister responsible for internal security and therefore (notionally at least) in charge of police and prisons, was at that time in a position of great trust. Tin Hlaing had been designated Chairman of the Myanmar Human Rights Committee, a government-run body that was openly

---

5   See foreignminister.gov.au/releases/2000/fa096_2000.html.
6   'Australian FM detects signs of movement from Myanmar', AFP, 24 July 2001.

envisaged as eventually being the precursor of an independent human rights commission under the Paris Principles for such bodies endorsed by the UN Human Rights Commission and the UN General Assembly.[7] So successful was this relatively modest exercise that the Australian Government had planned to launch a second, more intensive phase of the program in June 2003, but this was suspended because of the attack upon Aung San Suu Kyi and the NLD on 30 May 2003.

Interestingly, one of the more responsive organisations within the Ministry of Home Affairs was the Myanmar Police Force (MPF), whose International Division was quite well informed about international law enforcement issues ranging from human rights protection to counter-narcotics programs and people trafficking. Australia was not the only country engaging in direct cooperation with the MPF — the United Nations, the United States, and Japan also had specific law enforcement assistance programs — but Australia went further in treating Myanmar as a 'normal' jurisdiction that needed to conform with international norms. This went as far as inviting senior MPF officers, including the Director-General (or Chief of Police, Army Brigadier-General Soe Win), to visit Australia. There is no doubt at all that this was deeply appreciated by the MPF, who repeatedly displayed a highly cooperative and responsive attitude to proposals from the AFP. Australia's wholehearted cooperation with the MPF undoubtedly contributed to the MPF's ongoing commitment to improving Myanmar's conformity with international law enforcement norms across the board, but especially in reducing people trafficking, narcotics trafficking, and institutional discrimination against HIV/ AIDS sufferers.

---

7   See the section on 'Burma and Cambodia' in the DFAT Annual Report for 2000–01 which stated: 'Work on Mr Downer's Human Rights Institution initiative proceeded smoothly, with the first human rights training workshops held in July and October 2000. The workshops exposed middle-ranking Burmese civil servants to international human rights concepts, instruments and standards. An assessment by the workshop convenors concluded that the workshops had achieved their objectives, which included raising awareness of international human rights standards and obligations among Burmese officials and providing an opportunity for the Burmese participants to discuss human rights issues in an open manner.'

Acknowledging human rights abuses

At the government-to-government level, the Australian Government was extended considerable latitude in carrying out its controversial human rights training program with the Ministry of Home Affairs. Australian requests to carry out activities under the program were invariably approved, and the authorities studiously avoided interfering in the conduct of the training workshops, even though they were fully aware of the scope of the discussions and the extent to which Myanmar's human rights record was directly and indirectly challenged.[8] From the outset, Australia's human rights training program was a magnet for criticism of Australia, which had hoped that its limited engagement with the military regime could bring real results. This criticism came from Burmese activists and their supporters in Australia, who were never silent when it came to expressing their views and finding an opportunity to attack the military regime. Soon after the start of the program, Australian human rights lawyers (who were providing the training through the Castan Centre at Monash University) became targets for critical media commentary. Craig Skehan's September 2000 article in *The Age*, entitled 'Australian Rights Lawyers Under Fire on Burma', was fairly typical. Skehan wrote:

> Critics say the seminars are being used to pretend there is a willingness to reform while at the same time intensifying repression of dissent, including a crackdown this week on democracy leader Aung San Suu Kyi.[9]

Leader of the program, Professor David Kinley, was quoted as saying:

> The Burmese may be acting cynically, but I think there is at least a possibility of change … And I don't think these seminars in themselves are going to make the regime more palatable.

---

8   See a case study of the program by David Kinley and the author, 'Engaging a Pariah: Human Rights Training in Burma/Myanmar', *Human Rights Quarterly,* Vol. 29, No. 2, 2007. pp. 368–402.
9   Craig Skehan, 'Australian Rights Lawyers Under Fire on Burma', *The Age,* 6 September 2000.

Australia's human rights initiative was raised directly by Alexander Downer when he visited Myanmar in 2002. The US Embassy's report on a briefing I gave to like-minded ambassadors appeared in Wikileaks documents in 2012.[10]

From the beginning of 2000, the Australian Federal Police were able to develop satisfactory cooperation with the Ministry for Home Affairs and the Myanmar Police Force on anti-narcotics activity, and later on other areas of transnational crime, including people trafficking. Initially, capacity building training was focused on narcotics emanating from Burma.[11] Training was gradually extended to money laundering and people trafficking (the AFP's Southeast Asia regional program was for several years based in Yangon). One outcome regularly recognised in AFP public reporting was the decline in heroin production in Burma (the source of the bulk of Australia's illegal trafficking), which was in the view of the AFP attributable to the cooperation and trust developed with their counterparts. Australian (as well as US) anti-narcotics programs were implemented with what appeared to be full commitment and cooperation on the part of the Myanmar law enforcement authorities, despite the inherent sensitivity of some areas where SPDC authorities were sometimes under severe criticism (from the Burma lobby overseas, from conservative elements in the United States, and from certain circles in Thailand).

Law enforcement cooperation was extended to money laundering, and here the pattern of behaviour on the Myanmar side was similar, with Myanmar eventually being removed from the Financial Action Task Force black list of non-cooperating countries.[12] Australia was among

---

10   See cable 02rangoon1293, 'Downer Pushes Reform During Visit To Rangoon', October 2002. Available at wikileaks.org/plusd/cables/02RANGOON1293_a.html.

11   The AFP Annual Report for 2000–01 stated: 'The liaison officer in Yangon has forged an effective working relationship with the Burma Police and has provided vital intelligence and assistance to recent AFP offshore operations. Following the seizure of 357 kg of heroin in Fiji in October 2000, Burma authorities reacted to information provided by the AFP that led to the apprehension of the alleged organisers of the Fiji shipment. Through joint cooperation efforts the liaison officer and Burma police identified a second heroin shipment to Vanuatu, resulting in an additional offshore joint operation by the AFP with Vanuatu Police. The liaison officer in Yangon is also contributing to enhancing the law enforcement relations in the region, particularly between Burma and Thailand.'

12   This author's case study of the effectiveness of cooperation combined with compliance enforcement is in 'The Use of Normative Processes to Achieve Behaviour Change in Myanmar', in Nick Cheesman, Monique Skidmore and Trevor Wilson (eds), *Ruling Myanmar From Cyclone Nargis to National Elections*, Singapore: ISEAS Publications, 2010.

several Western donors urging the SPDC to introduce anti-money laundering laws. From Myanmar's point of view, there was no reason to hesitate. As it happened, the head of the Asia-Pacific regional group on money laundering at the time was an Australian, who visited Yangon to encourage the regime to take this step.

In another significant development, in July 2002 the Australian Government was successful in securing Myanmar Government agreement to carry out an assistance program to achieve harm reduction amongst intravenous drug users with HIV/AIDS. Such programs were controversial in many countries, even in Australia, and the Myanmar authorities approach to its own drug abusers was never especially tolerant or enlightened. But it was Ministry of Home Affairs officials, mainly key police officers in the Myanmar Police Force, who saw the value of such a program and were prepared to contemplate the 'harm reduction' program, which trialled needle exchanges for intravenous drug-users with HIV/AIDS. The program was launched at a press conference in Rangoon in July 2002.[13]

Subsequently, a major milestone in Australia's relations with Myanmar between 2000 and 2003 was Foreign Minister Alexander Downer's visit to Myanmar in October 2002, the first such visit in 19 years. The Japanese Foreign Minister, Yoriko Kawaguchi, was just ahead of him, visiting in August 2002. Not for the first time did Australian and Japanese policy approaches to Myanmar seem rather similar. Naturally, Downer was determined to meet both the head of state, Senior General Than Shwe, as well as Aung San Suu Kyi, who had been released from house arrest in May 2002. This was tantamount to officially recognising Aung San Suu Kyi as Leader of the Opposition, something the military regime did not explicitly do, although their behaviour towards her connoted as much. There was never much doubt that the regime would tolerate a meeting between Downer and Suu Kyi, as they had already allowed Foreign Minister Kawaguchi to meet her. From the regime's perspective, to receive a visit by a foreign minister from a government which had hitherto imposed sanctions on most government-to-government dealings was itself a point in their favour in terms of public perceptions.

---

13   Australian Embassy Rangoon Press Release, 5 July 2002.

Alexander Downer's personal expectations of the visit were quite modest and seemed realistic. Downer had explained the thinking behind his visit to Mark Baker of *The Age* as follows:

> Mr Downer said he believed Australia could influence the regime as it had maintained diplomatic contact in recent years and had provided limited humanitarian aid, including a controversial program of human rights courses for civil servants.
>
> 'Australia is of interest because we have taken a different, a unique approach in dealing with Myanmar (Burma),' he said. 'So we have contacts with them in a way that people like the British and the Americans at the other extreme don't have. We are perceived to be a so-called Western country, albeit a regional country ... and I think that gives us a bit more leverage than would otherwise be the case.'[14]

Nevertheless, some Australian journalists were quick to criticise him over the trip. Journalists' scepticism was reflected in the main ABC radio report, entitled 'Alexander Downer Gains Little from Burmese Meeting'.[15] It was stated more explicitly in Mark Baker's later report in *The Age:*

> Mr Downer also remains unapologetic about the maverick diplomacy that brought him to Rangoon — the most senior Western official to sit down with the regime in several years — while other Western governments continue to hold the junta at arm's length.
>
> He argues that a line should be drawn over Burma's brutal past and the role of those still in power. 'Going around blaming who's responsible for what's happened in the past, I can only say to you what's happened has happened, it can't be undone.
>
> 'Setting a commission of inquiry and pointing a finger at who's responsible for this isn't going to make any difference to history. We have to look to the future and hope that the future will be more productive than the past.
>
> Small comfort for the Burmese, still stuck in the tyranny that is their past and present.'[16]

---

14   Mark Baker, 'Suu Kyi Talks on the Way, Downer Told', *The Age*, 3 October 2002. Available at www.theage.com.au/articles/2002/10/02/1033538672884.html.

15   See the transcript of Eleanor Hall's interview on *The World Today* at www.abc.net.au/worldtoday/stories/s692508.htm.

16   See the full text of Baker's article, 'Downer Faces Burma's Tyrants', *The Age*, 5 October 2002. Available at www.theage.com.au/articles/2002/10/04/1033538774051.html.

Alexander Downer was the first Australian Foreign Minister to meet Aung San Suu Kyi. (His predecessor, Gareth Evans, had wanted to visit Myanmar and meet her, but this had not proved possible.) The Downer–Suu Kyi meeting occurred at her University Avenue residence, with no other NLD representative present. As might be expected, they took different positions in a 'vigorous' discussion of Australia's limited engagement, neither yielding to the other. Recalling their meeting much later, Downer was to describe Suu Kyi as 'downright aggressive'.[17]

From Australia's point of view — and especially from Alexander Downer's point of view — ensuring that Australian journalists could cover his visit was important. But the regime was unbending on this: they declined to give any Australian journalists a press visa, although one Australian journalist Mark Baker, who wrote for *The Age* and *The Sydney Morning Herald*, applied for a tourist visa and timed his travel so that he stayed for a period that overlapped with Downer. The Australian Embassy organised a press conference in the embassy at the end of the Downer visit, and although only certain Yangon-based journalists were permitted (by the regime) to attend, it was a relatively routine affair. Alexander Downer might have been concerned that a press conference held under the military regime's censorship would not be satisfactory, so he also gave a press conference about his visit to Myanmar when he arrived in Bangkok later the same day.

Overall, Downer's visit was publicly 'successful' — he was able to have substantive meetings with all those he wished to meet, and was able to get a good understanding of the main issues of the day — but it was not spectacularly so. In his own media release at the end of the visit, Downer said:

> At each of the meetings with Burmese leaders, I reinforced the need for early progress with the political reconciliation process and raised the consequences of delays in beginning substantive dialogue with Aung San Suu Kyi. Australia has welcomed the confidence-building process between the two parties which began in October 2000, but we believe that now is the time to begin the dialogue on issues such as constitutional reform.[18]

---

17   Article on 'Aung San Suu Kyi' in *The Advertiser* (Adelaide), May 2012.
18   Media Release, 'Burma Visit', 3 October 2002. See foreignminister.gov.au/releases/2002/fa144_02.html.

A dialogue on constitutional reform was, of course, impossible to pursue at that time. The military regime finalised its own draft constitution in 2006; it was submitted to a national referendum in May 2008, and enacted in March 2011. International lawyers from Australia conducted workshops on constitutional reform with their Myanmar counterparts in 2013–14 after reforms were begun.

Other Australian engagement programs

Alexander Downer was behind another important assistance initiative launched by Australia during this time, which proceeded when a satisfactory collaborative program design was arrived at with in principle support from the leading opposition party: a collaborative agricultural research program with technocratic arms of the Myanmar Government, to be conducted by the Australian Centre for International Agricultural Research (ACIAR). One unusual aspect of this program is that we were able to consult Aung San Suu Kyi as de facto Leader of the Opposition, as she happened to be at liberty when the ACIAR Program Manager was visiting, prior to finalising the design of the program. We informed the Ministry of Agriculture that we were doing this and they expressed no objection. Indeed, they might have even been pleased to get backing from Suu Kyi. (When Suu Kyi was able to travel around the country for the first time in many years in 2002–03, the first government project she visited was an irrigation project sponsored by the Ministry of Agriculture and Irrigation.) Aung San Suu Kyi saw no problem with this ACIAR program, provided that it was focused on the benefits it would bring to ordinary farmers, which was precisely the intention of the program anyway. However, it also involved strengthening the capacity of the Myanmar Government — in this case, the Myanmar Agriculture Service — which was something that other donors were still cautious about at that time.[19]

A second ACIAR project, providing technical assistance for the control of Newcastle disease in village chicken production systems, was launched in early 2003. The results of this project were very encouraging. The project report described the outcomes in the following terms:

---

19   See the ACIAR Press Release, 'Australia's first project in Burma', 9 April 2003, at aciar.gov. au/node/10357.

The capacity impacts of this project were remarkable, with training provided to local scientists in epidemiology, pathology, vaccine production, extension methods, and molecular assays … Poor farmers were the direct beneficiaries of this project — by improving the survival rate of young birds, more were available for sale at the markets and for consumption in the village households.[20]

Another project investigated pests in dryland agricultural crops.[21]

These initial agricultural research capacity building projects demonstrated that this could be a fruitful way of working with the technocratic arms of the Myanmar Government. Unfortunately, the 30 May 2003 Depayin incident, involving an attack on Aung San Suu Kyi's motorcade in Central Myanmar, led to the Australian Government suspending other ACIAR collaborative research proposals in Myanmar. The projects that had already started were allowed to be completed, but with slight delays.

There was no 'funeral service' for Australia's limited engagement policy with Myanmar. The human rights initiative, whose expansion into 2003 had been planned, was eventually suspended in response to the further detention of Daw Aung San Suu Kyi from June 2003 (which would last another seven years). I do not know whether Alexander Downer has any regrets over his Burma initiatives, but I am not aware of any public statement by him to this effect. I have not heard any objective criticisms of the human rights workshops after the event from other quarters. In Myanmar, Australia's readiness to undertake such initiatives is still recalled very positively more than a decade later.[22]

If there is any lasting 'legacy' from any of these initiatives, it could arguably be in the establishment — in the first term of the new government in 2011 — of a Myanmar National Human Rights Commission, including among its members several 'graduates' from the 2000–02 program, as well as the ongoing transnational crime capacity-

20   See the ACIAR project summary at aciar.gov.au/project/AH/2002/042.
21   See Heather Morris and D. F. Waterhouse, *The Distribution and Importance of Arthropod Pests and Weeds of Agriculture in Myanmar*, Canberra: ACIAR. Available at aciar.gov.au/files/node/2145/the_distribution_and_importance_of_arthropod_pests_48147.pdf.
22   In September/October 2012, the author was a member of an Australian team assessing the scope for new human rights capacity building in Myanmar which met many Myanmar participants in the original 2000–03 program, which they still praised.

building programs. (It is no accident that the Myanmar police officer most closely involved in international cooperation programs around this time, who was intimately associated with the Australian human rights workshops, Colonel Sit Aye, became international legal advisor to President Thein Sein in 2012.) Agricultural research collaboration on selected projects with different Myanmar Government research establishments aimed at improving productivity and grass-roots outreach continues to this day.

Some opportunistic actions for increasing engagement

Occasionally, the Australian Embassy had opportunities to encourage further international engagement by the military regime, either to 'fill gaps' in Myanmar's compliance with international norms, or to press the regime into 'normalising' Myanmar's international policies, including adhering to the International Covenant on Civil and Political Rights. Although we were told by the Ministry of Home Affairs in 2001 that a working group had been set up to consider the question of Myanmar adhering to the International Covenant on Civil and Political Rights, we did not hear the outcome of this work before the suspension of Australian human rights workshops in 2003. Myanmar has still not signed and ratified this convention more than 10 years later.

Compliance with universal international arms control agreements was another obvious area to try to seek more conformity with international norms. Any improvement in Myanmar's conformity with such instruments would contribute to regional security. By 2000, Myanmar was already participating in the ASEAN Regional Forum, which undertook a range of regional security confidence-building measures.[23] Thus we encouraged Myanmar to adhere to the International Landmines Convention, in view of evidence of the widespread use of landmines in Myanmar. The Myanmar Government never agreed to take this step, which would have (by design) constrained the Burmese

23   One area of ASEAN Regional Forum activity where Myanmar was slow to adopt a proactive position was the desirability of issuing a regular comprehensive statement of defence policy and weapons holdings.

army's use of landmines. But they did allow the ICRC to conduct a program to treat civilians with landmine injuries, and allowed the Mines Action Group to carry out an Australian Government-funded 'landmines awareness' education program in 2002.

We also encouraged the regime to allow Amnesty International to visit Myanmar and interview prisoners of conscience. Amnesty International's highly effective mobilisation of communities around the world to campaign for the release of political prisoners received enormous support around Australia. (Even the Amnesty International group in my own home town of Kiama, NSW, was lobbying for the release of Burmese prisoners of conscience.) At that time, Amnesty International's Bangkok Office was actively monitoring the situation of political prisoners, who were already being visited by the ICRC. We were told by Donna Guest from the Amnesty International Bangkok Office that they would be prepared to visit Myanmar for the first time, if invited and given access to prisoners. Donna Guest visited Myanmar in 2002 and 2003.[24]

We also urged Myanmar to consider signing the Comprehensive Test Ban Treaty, to reinforce their commitment under the Nuclear Non-Proliferation Treaty not to develop nuclear arms. They never did this, although they continued to comply with International Atomic Energy Agency safeguards procedures. Myanmar signed the Nuclear Non-Proliferation Treaty Additional Protocol in 2013, but has yet to ratify the instrument. Myanmar has signed, but not ratified, the Comprehensive Nuclear Test Ban Treaty.

At a time when climate change was at the forefront of international agendas, but the environment was not a high priority in Myanmar, the Australian Embassy encouraged Myanmar to follow what was happening in international climate change developments. We did this by taking advantage of a private visit to Myanmar by a senior officer from the Australian Department of the Environment, arranging for him to brief Myanmar Government officials on international climate change developments. It was relatively easy to do this through the Ministry of Foreign Affairs, which coincidentally had formal responsibility for

---

24   Amnesty International, 'Media Report on First Visit to Myanmar'. See www.asiantribune. com/news/2003/02/10/amnesty-internationalits-first-myanmar-visit.

climate change issues. The briefing was well attended, but it would be another 10 years before Myanmar had a Ministry for the Environment (under President Thein Sein).

The Ministry of Foreign Affairs was also interested to find out about the operations of the Asia-Pacific Economic Cooperation (APEC) organisation. Although there was little prospect then of Myanmar becoming a member, we saw no problem with providing them with information about this Australian initiative, which we did each time APEC met. Myanmar is still not a member of APEC, but it did host the East Asian Summit in 2014.

8
Encounters with Daw Aung San Suu Kyi

During the early 2000s, there were opportunities to have substantive contact with the best-known and most impressive politician in Myanmar, Daw Aung San Suu Kyi, whose party, the National League for Democracy (NLD), had won an overwhelming majority of the seats in the only recent elections in 1990, and who had never been charged with any offence under the law, but was regularly placed under house arrest. Usually, neither she nor the NLD were able to carry out normal political activities of any kind, even though the NLD was legally registered as a political party and had not been banned by the State Peace and Development Council (SPDC). For its part, the military regime (especially its leader from 1994–2011, Senior General Than Shwe) pursued policies towards Aung San Suu Kyi and the NLD that were often contradictory and which swung dramatically from tightening restrictions against her in September 2000 to engaging in (secret) talks in January 2001, before releasing her completely in May 2002.

Suu Kyi's party, the NLD, was basically a coalition of left-leaning groups and military leaders who had fallen out with the mainstream of the army. It was formed to compete in the 1990 elections, and was still an officially registered party until 2010, when it split over whether to contest the 2010 elections. Even as a legal political party, the NLD was under constant pressure from the authorities, who constantly monitored NLD members' movements and activities, subjected members to various forms of low-level harassment, and actively sought to pressure them to leave the party. Judging by the propaganda in the official media, the authorities seemed to be locked into a campaign to reduce membership of and support for the NLD to the point where it could not compete with a government-organised political party. After 1990, NLD members were systematically harassed and persecuted by military authorities, and many were jailed, often on spurious or technical grounds. Between 2000 and 2002, the authorities consistently mounted public campaigns to pressure NLD members to resign from the party.

During the period 1995–2000, members of the Yangon diplomatic community could have considerable access to Aung San Suu Kyi. While she was not under house arrest but was restricted to Yangon, it was still possible to meet her occasionally, but not frequently, by requesting an appointment through the Myanmar Government. At other times, when the provisions of her house arrest were tightened, no diplomats were able to meet her. Through these years, ambassadors from Western countries and Japan never stopped trying to preserve the minimal contacts they could have with Suu Kyi and the NLD leadership. Other ambassadors — from Asian countries such as China and India, and elsewhere — were noticeable for not seeking to meet her. It was very difficult, however, to convince some of the ASEAN ambassadors that they should make a point of meeting her — the Philippines Ambassador being an exception. All conversations with Suu Kyi were probably bugged by Myanmar's intelligence agency, but this did not necessarily prevent frank and full discussions. In my meetings with Suu Kyi, she did not overtly display any concern about being eavesdropped on — it was simply assumed that this happened.

Writing more than 10 years later, with so many recent changes in Myanmar, it is hard to envisage how comprehensively and cruelly Aung San Suu Kyi was isolated from her own people and the rest of the world by the Myanmar authorities. For most of the time, the only communication she had was her short-wave radio, which she used to listen to the BBC. For most of the time, she did not have use of a telephone; the NLD Headquarters had a phone, but it was often not functioning. She did not have access to the internet and satellite TV broadcasts until after her release from detention in late 2010. The NLD itself was not permitted to have a website until early 2011. As far as I know, Aung San Suu Kyi still does not have or use a mobile phone.

Her isolation between the late 1980s and 2010 was extremely severe. Very few Myanmar people were allowed to visit her, apart from her own staff, her doctor Tin Myo Win (Douglas), and her long-standing lawyer at that time, U Kyi Win (Neville, who is now deceased). Her two sons were living in the UK and were only rarely permitted to visit her in Myanmar. Her older brother, Aung San Oo, with whom she is not close, is a US citizen and lives in the United States.

While fiercely challenging the restrictions on her whenever she could, Aung San Suu Kyi was careful not to step over the line and give the military regime any excuse to take more drastic action against her. So there was always an element of pragmatism, mixed with principle, in her approach. She occasionally met foreign journalists at this time, but was always extremely cautious in what she said to them. Visiting journalists, somewhat in her thrall, may not have always understood the subtlety of her position. However, Suu Kyi's position on political negotiations with the military regime during this period was not especially flexible or successful: she always insisted on a 'dialogue' with the NLD and ethnic groups as a first step in the process of political reconciliation, when it was apparent that the military would not treat her as an equal, and would not elevate or enhance her political standing with the ethnic groups. She always sought to deal directly with regime head Senior General Than Shwe, who was not known for being flexible, open-minded, or well disposed towards her. She rarely raised 'reconciliation' as a goal, which the military might have found harder to object to than 'negotiations'. She generally avoided specifying any particular topic or issue as being one on which the NLD held an incontrovertible position. She gave the impression that she did not recognise or accept that she was not in a position to call the shots, and she would never settle for anything else. Meanwhile, she confronted the regime most vigorously on issues such as her ability to travel, and (not unreasonably) her personal access to lawyers and doctors. Only rarely did she identify a substantive issue or problem as requiring the regime to listen to her views. In other words, the ingredients for a perpetual stand-off between the two principal protagonists were fixed by both sides, and had scarcely moved since 1990.

Fortunate good access

Normally, a new ambassador could seek a meeting with Aung San Suu Kyi after presenting credentials to the head of state and making an introductory call on the Minister for Foreign Affairs. Military intelligence would decide whether or not to permit and facilitate a meeting, which normally took place at her University Avenue residence. Even this process meant a certain amount of contact between Suu Kyi and the military regime. It was never entirely clear who was responsible for approving the meeting, and whether or not it took place promptly. My first meeting with Suu Kyi in 2000 was arranged through this process, and I do not recall any delays or issues. She had known several of my predecessors, and through them and a few Australians who managed to visit her, seemed to have a high regard for Australia, although not for the Australian Government's initiatives seeking limited engagement with the military regime. The titular head of the NLD at this time, Chairman U Aung Shwe, was a former Ambassador to Australia, so Australian connections with the NLD were good, although not nearly as close as those between Suu Kyi and the US and UK governments.

It was normal at this time for ambassadors of those countries who gave moral support to the NLD to attend occasional important meetings organised by them at party headquarters at Shwegonedine Road in Yangon. Suu Kyi might attend such meetings, but it was not normally possible to talk to NLD leaders on such occasions. On other occasions, it was sometimes possible to arrange meetings with other members of the NLD Central Executive Committee, such as Chairman U Aung Shwe, Deputy Chairman U Tin Oo, and party spokesman U Lwin. It was never easy to meet NLD leaders under such circumstances, but it was possible if one persevered. Some embassies — mainly those from ASEAN and nearby Asian countries — never attempted to meet NLD leaders, on the grounds that the military regime did not want such contacts to occur. Interestingly, when UN Special Envoy Razali Ismail paid his first visit in the middle of 2000, he sought my assistance to arrange (and provide a venue for) his first meeting with the leadership of the NLD. With Canberra's agreement, that meeting with NLD Deputy Chair Tin Oo took place at the Australian Ambassador's residence in June 2000.[1]

Obviously, under such restrictions, Suu Kyi had very limited or no contact with her supporters abroad — whether Burmese pro-democracy activists in exile, of whom there were several hundred thousand, including a government-in-exile, the National Coalition Government of the Union of Burma (NCGUB),[2] led by Suu Kyi's cousin, Dr Sein Win, or foreign supporters such as the Burma Campaigns in the United States, the UK, and Australia. The NCGUB included a number of NLD members who had been elected in the 1990 elections, a few of whom had permanent residence status in Australia. Suu Kyi rarely touched on her interest in or contacts with Australia in conversations with me; it is not clear whether or not this was deliberate. A number of Australians and Burmese living in Australia purported to be loyal supporters, and followed Suu Kyi's actions and words very closely. (Many young Burmese in Australia were strong NLD supporters, but many older Burmese-born residents of Australia were disinterested in politics.)

When discussing political developments, Suu Kyi always spoke carefully and deliberately, and was usually prepared to cover a wide range of topics. She seemed fully committed to the domestic and international efforts to achieve political reconciliation in Myanmar, even though the prospects for success did not seem high and she was not necessarily negotiating from a position of obvious strength. She never disguised her profound mistrust of the military regime, but did not needlessly pursue unrealistic political goals. Despite the gloomy situation facing the country and its people, she was essentially optimistic about her own role and the future. She did not seem unduly concerned that reform in Myanmar would probably not be achieved without considerable international support, and indeed

1   I had known Razali previously when we were both serving as diplomats in Vientiane, and while the UN's Yangon Office could have easily arranged this meeting for Razali, he preferred to operate independently to a certain extent. He obviously would not ask the military regime to arrange his meeting with Aung San Suu Kyi, nor did the Malaysian Embassy have the necessary contacts. After this, Razali met Suu Kyi in her residence in programs arranged for him by the Myanmar authorities.
2   Until February 2000, Amanda Zappia had been the NCGUB's official representative in Australia.

often explained how she thought this international support should be mobilised and channelled. The central tenet of her approach at this time was a call for 'genuine dialogue' with the military leadership, but she tended not to espouse specific, detailed policies.

Naturally, Suu Kyi herself deeply resented the conditions of the unjustifiable restrictions placed on her by the regime, without any charges being brought against her, and without any court imposing such measures, since she and the NLD had not committed any offences. In fact, these were measures imposed under martial law, although this was not often stated publicly. One effect of Suu Kyi's continuous objection to these restrictions during the period 1998–May 2002 were her endless attempts to assert her basic rights, to defy the authorities, and to travel outside Yangon. These sometimes led to rather theatrical confrontations in odd circumstances, such as her being held for several days on a bridge on the outskirts of Yangon in 1998 and again in 2000, and being refused a ticket on the train to Mandalay in 2000 (which was the reason she was returned to house arrest in August 2000). These were examples of bravery and fierce civil disobedience on the part of Suu Kyi, but they were also humiliating, risky, and had somewhat unpredictable consequences. They did not seem to achieve any concrete outcomes, but did gain considerable international publicity (but not domestically, because of the tight censorship imposed over domestic media). When these incidents occurred, Australia and other pro-democratic countries were mostly concerned about Suu Kyi's well-being (although there was not much we could do on her behalf) and for the possibility of the situation escalating out of control.

Being put in one's place by an 'icon'

After Aung San Suu Kyi was released from house arrest through the intervention of UN Special Envoy Razali Ismail in May 2002, it was possible to maintain something closer to a normal relationship with her. Appointments could be arranged directly and as frequently as was mutually convenient, and it was possible to invite her to functions at embassies. In 2000, the Australian Embassy arranged for a working lunch for Suu Kyi at the Australian Ambassador's residence with representatives of the non-government humanitarian organisations that were run from Australia: World Vision, and CARE. Before this,

Suu Kyi had not had opportunities to talk to INGOs about their work in Myanmar. It seemed important that they have a chance to meet her and hear her views, and that she have the same opportunity to find out how they operated on the ground. The lunch went smoothly enough and achieved its purposes. I recall that Suu Kyi fiercely criticised one of the Burmese INGO staff guests (whom she was meeting for the first time) for, in effect, collaborating with the military regime, criticism that was both inaccurate and unfair. Indeed, Suu Kyi interrogated one of the World Vision Burmese female staff so intensely that the woman (a doctor) was reduced to tears.

Under any circumstances, Aung San Suu Kyi would be an impressive person to meet, and much has been said and written about meetings with her. As with others who met her, Suu Kyi's presence, poise, and personality left a deep impression on me. She knows other Australians, and considers Australia to be one of the countries strongly supporting her, both through the Burmese diaspora, and through political and other connections. So she attached some importance to what Australia did in relation to Myanmar, even though she was yet to visit Australia. Her unfailing politeness does not disguise her genuine appreciation for Australian efforts to help the Burmese people, although she might not always agree with every aspect of official Australian policy. She seems to enjoy having unquestioning US and UK support, and would notice the difference in the attitudes of Australian Government leaders. (The Australian Labor Party is probably more disposed to hold up Suu Kyi as a figure of authority, given the close-to-fraternal ties it has with the NLD.) Recalling some years later his own encounter with Suu Kyi in October 2002, Alexander Downer described her as 'feisty and surprisingly aggressive'.[3]

Suu Kyi let it be known quite bluntly that she did not think such INGOs were doing enough to fight against unreasonable or restrictive practices imposed on them by the Myanmar authorities at the expense of the interests and well-being of ordinary people. She believed that most INGOs would do whatever was necessary to stay in Myanmar, even if this meant violating their own principles and offending basic proprieties. However, at that time, Suu Kyi and the NLD did not fully understand the difficult situation faced by INGO staff; they certainly

3   Alexander Downer, 'Burma's Agent of Change', *The Advertiser*, 1 April 2012. Available at www. adelaidenow.com.au/archive/news/downer-burmas-agent-of-change/story-e6freacl-1226315903405.

did not realise the lengths that INGO staff, such as those at World Vision, went to quite frequently in order to rescue young Burmese boys who had been recruited against their will as child soldiers. Certainly, under the military regime INGOs had not been allowed to carry out overt political activities, while the NLD's contact with foreigners had not been encouraged.

If I had a particular need to talk to Aung San Suu Kyi about a work matter, the routine was to phone the NLD office to request an appointment. Suu Kyi normally agreed to such requests for a meeting, and I would inform DFAT in Canberra when a meeting with her was scheduled. I do not recall receiving much in the way of guidance or instructions from DFAT ahead of meetings with Suu Kyi. On the whole, it was not necessary to receive detailed 'spoon feeding' before meeting her; some elements of conversations with her were taken for granted: the state of her relations with the regime, her views on the overall political situation, any particular issues or requests she might have, and her views on any specific Australia-related matters. Suu Kyi would respond directly on any matters raised: she was quite comfortable sharing her views on the regime, which were predictably critical, and founded on deep mistrust and suspicion; she would speak with authority on NLD policy, but rarely, if ever, acknowledged any faults on the part of the NLD; she was always full of praise for the NLD and her supporters inside the country, but was noticeably less enthusiastic about her overseas supporters, Burmese or foreign, whom she did not often mention; and she never complained about her personal situation, and would not normally touch on her own health or well-being. On the other hand, she tended to be quite tight-lipped about her dealings with the military regime, and never disclosed confidential discussions with UN envoys or other high-level visitors.

Suu Kyi responded to a request from me for a meeting by saying that she would be happy to call on my wife at the ambassador's residence for afternoon tea, and if I wished to drop in, that was up to me. Years later, Suu Kyi would always show fondness for my wife, and when Suu Kyi visited The Australian National University in November 2013 to receive an honorary degree, my wife (a graduate and former employee of ANU) attended the meeting between Suu Kyi and ANU academic staff, and there is a memorable photograph by an ANU photographer of Suu Kyi embracing my wife at one break during the meeting.

We had one other form of regular contact with Aung San Suu Kyi, which was not 'authorised' by anyone. My wife kept (at our own expense) some 20 chickens in a chicken pen inside the extensive grounds of the ambassador's residence. The chickens produced more eggs than we could possibly eat, so we offered some to Aung San Suu Kyi on a regular basis, as we knew she was supporting a large number of people at her residence. The arrangement was that our private driver would deliver eggs to Suu Kyi's University Avenue residence once a week. After a while, our private car would be recognised as it approached her gate and allowed to pass through unchecked with its valuable consignment. Our driver was delighted to be able to do this, and Suu Kyi was always effusive in her thanks for the eggs. Of course, I assume other well-wishers were also helping Suu Kyi and the NLD in comparable ways, but I never asked about this.

In conversation, Suu Kyi was usually relaxed and showed her wide interests — from domestic affairs to grand policy. But she was always conscious that any comment she made would be passed on and could take on wider importance, and she gave the impression that everything she said was very carefully calculated. She was quick to correct any loose wording or generalised comments. She was always contemptuous and mistrustful of the military regime, and did not seem to have much regard for members of the Myanmar bureaucracy who were prepared to work for it. She did not hide her admiration for the US and the UK, who gave her unstinting support. She was never disrespectful of the United Nations, although it was sometimes clear that she did not always place much confidence in them to assist her cause. Her attitude to the Burmese diaspora was interesting: she was obviously grateful for their great dedication and commitment, but often expressed views slightly at variance from what the pro-democracy activists were saying. However, she was careful not to criticise or openly disagree with them.

Although she assumed a modest manner, and was not boastful or pompous, she was very conscious of her own importance, was naturally formal and courteous by nature, and came across as rather proper. But she also had a sense of humour, and often joked about some of the circumstances she had to face. Suu Kyi was not impressed by the Australian-run *Myanmar Times*, which she would have regarded as an apologist for the regime and altogether too close to military intelligence. Suu Kyi could, however, be prickly to deal with, and I was certainly not alone in experiencing this. Most written accounts about her tend to reflect an obvious hagiographic perspective, but even the most detailed biography by British writer Justin Wintle mentions Suu Kyi giving insincere people 'short shrift'.[4] Quite a few Australians interested in Burma would have met her, and some claimed to be in regular communication with her.

Consulting Aung San Suu Kyi as 'Leader of the Opposition'

When Aung San Suu Kyi was free to travel and meet whomever she wished, it was natural to view her as the de facto Leader of the Opposition and therefore the person to be consulted about any policy matters or initiatives that were being considered by foreign governments. The US and the UK (who gained more frequent access to her than any other embassies) took this to the ultimate extent, and effectively gave Suu Kyi a veto over their policies towards Myanmar. This was particularly galling for the military regime (as it was intended to be), but it also reduced the flexibility the Americans and British had in pursuing their Burma policies. If Suu Kyi could not make up her mind over an issue, US and UK policies could be frozen instead of adjusting flexibly. Their approach also invested Suu Kyi with a degree of infallibility, which most Burmese would not have ascribed to her even at the time, and almost certainly not in 2013.

Australian Governments did not go this far, nor did most other governments. This meant that while we had good and supportive relations with Aung San Suu Kyi, there was sometimes an element of tension if Australia was attempting something that Suu Kyi did not approve of. Australia's human rights capacity-building workshops were a good example of this. In October 2002, *The Age* journalist Mark Baker was able to interview Aung San Suu Kyi shortly after Alexander Downer's visit to Yangon. Baker's report — carried in *The Age* under the headline 'Suu Kyi Attacks Canberra' — quoted Aung San Suu Kyi as saying:

---

4   Justin Wintle, *Perfect Hostage: A Life of Aung San Suu Kyi*, London: Hutchinson, 2007.

Australia should endorse a tough regime of sanctions imposed by the United States and the European Union and limit its contacts with the regime until it honoured promises to start talks on political reform. She described a controversial Australian program of human rights training courses for Burmese officials as pointless and a waste of money.[5]

Baker — who had been unable to obtain a journalist's visa for the Downer visit in 2002, despite the Australian Embassy's interventions with the Myanmar authorities to allow Australian journalists to cover the visit — describes Aung San Suu Kyi's views as a 'rebuke' to Alexander Downer. Afterwards, this article was not directly raised with Aung San Suu Kyi: it did not help Australia with the Burma lobby in Australia, nor did it particularly help Aung San Suu Kyi in Myanmar or with international agencies who had publicly supported this Australian program. At that time, Baker's article would not have been seen by many Burmese in Myanmar at all.

Aung San Suu Kyi had previously discussed Australia's human rights training program with former Australian Human Rights Commissioner Chris Sidoti when he visited Myanmar in 1999.[6] Suu Kyi was invited to meet with the Australian training team of human rights experts (David Kinley, Chris Sidoti, and Kate Eastman) again in 2002 over lunch at the Australian Ambassador's residence.[7] On this occasion, she made it clear that she did not like this program, as in her view it would provide 'cover' for the military regime without reducing human rights abuses, and because the program would not include the main perpetrators of human rights abuses, the army. She was not at all convinced Australian experts' accounts of the free hand they were given to tackle any human rights issues head on, or by the indications they recounted of officials and law enforcement officers finding value in the workshops' treatment of human rights issues that were directly relevant to them, such as interrogation of prisoners, or treatment of prison inmates. She was not at all uncomfortable telling the rare visiting Australian journalist about her misgivings.

---

5   Mark Baker, 'Suu Kyi Attacks Canberra', *The Age*, 7 October 2002.
6   Craig Skehan, 'Suu Kyi Warming to Rights Seminars', *Sydney Morning Herald*, 20 February 2001.
7   The fourth team member, then at Monash University, and alternating as a trainer, was Dr Sarah Joseph.

There was at least one other opportunity where it was possible to consult Suu Kyi in a low-key way about a new Australian Government initiative. This was the proposal by Australian Foreign Minister Alexander Downer to provide agricultural research assistance to Myanmar through the Australian Centre for International Agricultural Research (ACIAR).[8] When the head of ACIAR's International Project Branch, Allan Barden, was visiting Yangon in late 2002 for initial discussions about this proposal with the Myanmar Government, it seemed sensible to consult Suu Kyi about the proposal as well, since the visit coincided with her movements being unrestricted. Suu Kyi naturally took this in her stride and listened carefully as the proposal was outlined. She said she could see the benefits of the project, and, fortunately, did not express any objection to the proposal (as we had not asked DFAT directly about consulting Suu Kyi on the idea). Her only comment was to urge that the project at all times keep the interests of the Myanmar villagers uppermost. This was indeed precisely the way ACIAR projects were carried out, and this particular project (about rodent infestation of rice crops) was exemplary in being embedded in grass-roots needs.[9]

The Australian Embassy briefed Suu Kyi on the Australian Federal Police's engagement in capacity building and law enforcement cooperation with the Myanmar Government as part of broader anti-narcotics cooperation arrangements. This cooperation later expanded to other areas of transnational crime, such as money laundering and people trafficking. Suu Kyi was generally supportive of such programs. If she had misgivings about the Myanmar Police Force as one of the arms of Myanmar's successive authoritarian regimes — occasionally bringing them into conflict with her — she did not allow these views to colour her reaction to such programs. Such Australian Embassy meetings with Aung San Suu Kyi mostly took place at NLD Headquarters at Shwegonedine, and a few other NLD leaders might also participate. Meetings at her University Avenue residence were more unusual, and reserved for high-level visitors such as Alexander Downer. But at those brief times when she was free, it was not unusual to meet her at other functions and venues.

---

8   Alexander Downer had previously tried the same idea on another apparently impenetrable regime, the Democratic Republic of Korea, with some success.
9   Media Release, 'ACIAR's first project in Burma', 9 August 2003.

The Australian Embassy had always maintained regular friendly contacts with the NLD leadership: Suu Kyi herself if and when that was possible; U Aung Shwe, Chairman, and former Ambassador to Australia; U Tin Oo, Deputy Chair; U Kyi Maung, Central Executive Committee member; and U Lwin, Spokesman. Telephone communications with the NLD were often interrupted, and the NLD had neither fax nor (at that time) email facilities. Visits to the rather dilapidated NLD head office in the Shwegonedine area of Yangon under full scrutiny of police and intelligence guards were not uncommon. I once tried unsuccessfully to visit the large NLD office in Mandalay. Regime harassment of the NLD and its members was quite systematic and severe throughout 2000–03. I observed NLD offices that had been opened in Mawlamyaing and Indaw (Sagaing Division), but I was admonished by an official guide for photographing a (closed) NLD office in Mogok in early 2003.

During May 2002–May 2003, although Aung San Suu Kyi was notionally free to receive visitors, the military regime still tried to discourage contact with her. Of course, they could not normally prevent UN envoys or ASEAN envoys from meeting her, even when her movements were restricted. (They did manage to dampen down media briefings being given in Yangon about these meetings.) I recall only one situation where Aung San Suu Kyi participated in discussions with the Yangon diplomatic community at which she was essentially treated as Leader of the Opposition. This was a meeting between the international donors and NGOs about HIV/AIDS, which had been publicly proposed by UN Special Representative Razali Ismail as a potential field for cooperation between the military regime and the NLD. The meeting was uneventful. It was more an exchange of views than anything else. Suu Kyi did not dominate the discussions and was very attentive when experts were providing their views. The NLD had been somewhat more 'progressive' on the issue of HIV/AIDS compared to the military regime, and had opened its own HIV/AIDS 'Prevention and Treatment Centre' as early as 2002, but had not really sought to make HIV/AIDS a differentiating issue.[10] However, the idea of some partnership between the military regime and the NLD on a 'national emergency' issue such as HIV/AIDS did not progress

---

10   An International Crisis Group 'Asia Briefing' in December 2004 described the NLD attitude to the HIV/AIDS crisis at that time.

and was eventually dropped. There was never any indication that the Than Shwe regime was prepared to pursue even such a limited 'power sharing' experiment at that time. But, more than a decade later, this is exactly what has happened under the Thein Sein Government, which invited Suu Kyi to participate in parliamentary activities on the Rohingya communal violence issue and on rule of law generally.

Dealings with Aung San Suu Kyi about the political situation were always interesting, and she was always happy to discuss important policy matters, but she could be quite evasive when it suited her. For example, she gave away very little about her ongoing talks with the military regime, which until the end she maintained did not constitute the two-way dialogue among equals that she had in mind. One generally hesitated to offer her advice, as she had usually formed her views on issues. The strong undertone of nationalism underlying her views was sometimes unexpected, but should not have been surprising. For example, she was inordinately proud of Burmese achievements of any kind, and once said, when acknowledging the special role the Burmese military would always play in Myanmar, that she would expect the Burmese army to beat the Thai army in any contest of military power. This was before the 2002 border clashes with Thailand, in which the *Tatmadaw* performed poorly against their Thai counterparts. She made it clear that she has a soft spot for younger people, but equally always spoke with genuine respect for the elderly 'uncles' with whom she shared the leadership of the NLD.

Suu Kyi's supporters and detractors

Like other ambassadors in Yangon at this time, I occasionally met several of Suu Kyi's advisors, including her doctor, Tin Myo Win (Douglas), and her lawyers, all of whom were subjected to severe and entirely gratuitous harassment by the authorities. They were all brave, loyal, and totally committed supporters, usually very discreet and careful in what they said, even to diplomats. All admired and respected Suu Kyi enormously and were extremely dedicated to working with her. Sometimes, however, they admitted to having some differences of opinion with Suu Kyi. Her economic advisor, the former Myanmar diplomat and UN economist, U Myint, sometimes mentioned having problems convincing her of the rationale for his economic views, and much later (after 2012) would lose influence with her. Some of Suu Kyi's other advisors would remain loyal to her, including after her election to parliament in April 2012.

One elected member of the NLD who spoke openly of his personal disagreement with Suu Kyi was U Ohn Maung, who was elected as an MP for Inle Lake in Shan State in 1990, and who, like most other NLD MPs, was subsequently arrested for his political activities. After his release from gaol, in the early 2000s Ohn Maung became the proprietor of the Inle Princess Hotel, one of the first of the new generation of tourist hotels on the shore of Inle Lake. Ohn Maung, whose health had been seriously affected by his treatment in prison, spoke of disagreeing with Suu Kyi about the attempts by some in the West to impose bans on tourism to Myanmar. Ohn Maung of course did not agree with this, and said that he failed in his attempts to persuade Suu Kyi of the direct and indirect benefits of tourism for the local people. He always maintained that human rights abuses in Shan State, and around Inle Lake in particular, had decreased noticeably after tourists began coming to the area. Suu Kyi was disposed to support the tourism ban, although she was sometimes careful how she spoke publicly about this. There were never really good arguments for banning tourism, which directly and indirectly benefited local people and the local economies.

Amongst the general public, as far as one could tell in a country that had no opinion polls at that time, Suu Kyi did indeed enjoy remarkable popular support and popularity. It was hard to assess the extent of support the NLD and Suu Kyi had amongst the bureaucracy, as they were not permitted to have anything to do with her, or to mention her name (hence the euphemism 'the Lady'). One would expect that a large number of bureaucrats would have supported her. When she was released from house arrest in May 2002 and was quickly giving interviews at a press conference, I was speaking by phone to a senior bureaucrat in his office during working hours and was surprised when he made it clear that he was watching the CNN coverage of her release by satellite broadcast in his office and described it to me as 'great news'.

On the other hand, the Burmese army was widely said to 'hate' Suu Kyi. Working in Yangon at this time, one certainly often heard members of the military (even the Office of Strategic Studies) speaking critically of Suu Kyi, but this was often a public expression of what they were expected to say (or what they had been trained to say). There is no reason to think that no members of the military supported or even admired Suu Kyi and the NLD, but neither is there any basis to think that this would translate into an internal rift in the army. Suu Kyi herself sometimes spoke quite favourably of the military intelligence liaison officers with whom she dealt regularly.

More generally, I met several Burmese not connected to the military regime but involved in politics who openly claimed that they did not agree with Suu Kyi, did not have a high opinion of the NLD, and believed that the NLD was not the best political alternative. Indeed, it was rather surprising to encounter quite a lot of Burmese who individually believed that unswerving Western support for the NLD was not the best option for Myanmar. It was also common among ethnic groups to find a considerable degree of doubt about Suu Kyi and the NLD — they commonly questioned whether she knew and understood ethnic concerns, and doubted that she really had ethnic interests at heart. One example I encountered directly was the Kachin Independence Organisation (KIO) leadership at the time, who in 2002 had still not met Suu Kyi, and asked whether I thought they should do so.[11] Naturally, I encouraged them to set up a meeting with her, which I understand they subsequently did. However, it was notable that in some cases where Burmese had appeared publicly to turn against Suu Kyi, they were subject to campaigns of abuse and criticism in the pro-democratic media.[12]

Journalists, diplomats, and foreigners who had opportunities to meet and know Suu Kyi were uniformly impressed by her personality, her charisma, her poise, her commitment, and her broad command of issues. It was normal to hear more fulsome praise and endorsement of Suu Kyi's views from Americans and Europeans than from Burmese. Most Americans and Europeans were not really objective in their

---

11   I had met the then KIO leader Saboi Jum both in Yangon and Myitkina, and I assumed he was checking with many people before he took a possibly risky step, which could arouse the SPDC's ire.

12   I have in mind the case of the journalist, Ma Thein Gi, who had for a time in the 1990s been personal assistant to Aung San Suu Kyi.

reactions to her. This contrasts with the views one might hear from Australians, who seemed more prepared to mention her inflexibility, stubbornness, and occasionally questionable political judgment.[13]

Meeting again 10 years later

Almost 10 years later, in late 2010, I received an unexpected telephone call from the Department of Foreign Affairs and Trade's Vietnam, Cambodia and Myanmar Director asking me for details of my last meeting with Aung San Suu Kyi in early 2003. It transpired that Suu Kyi was about to be released from house arrest and the Australian Chargé d'Affaires was to be among the diplomats she would meet on her release (at her request). However, in the intervening years since my last meeting with her at a private social function in Yangon in April 2003, none of the succeeding Australian ambassadors had met Suu Kyi; it had just not been possible for them to do so, as she had been under house arrest informally or formally for all of that time. I had not been able to bid her farewell, as she was attacked and arrested on 30 May 2003 just before the end of my assignment. I wrote her a farewell letter before my departure from Myanmar the following month, June 2003, but she almost certainly would not have received it.

I had met Aung San Suu Kyi next when I visited Myanmar in September 2012, when I was a member of an unofficial Australian human rights delegation. That meeting actually took place in the new capital, Naypyitaw, as she was by then an elected member of parliament.)

In November 2013, Aung San Suu Kyi would finally visit Australia for the first time, and was awarded an honorary doctorate of letters at ANU, when my wife and I met her again.

During her visit to the east coast of Australia, much larger numbers of the Burmese community than expected attended functions in Suu Kyi's honour in Canberra, Sydney, and Melbourne, and it was apparent that many Burmese who were not necessarily politically involved nevertheless admired her and were keen to see her in the flesh. So, whether at home or overseas, she commanded enormous respect and affection from ordinary Burmese people.

---

13   A good example is Hazel Lang's frank 2006 article, 'The Courage of Aung San Suu Kyi', *Overland,* Issue 183, Winter 2006.

9

Bilateral Sanctions and Successful Alternative Approaches

Australia was one of a number of 'like-minded', largely Western (or OECD) countries that imposed political and military (and later economic) 'sanctions' against 'Burma' or Myanmar. But these were not mandatory, universally applied sanctions authorised by the UN Security Council. This meant that Australia was not aligned with the majority of countries with official relations with Myanmar, but in a small, but powerful, group of countries with a political or even ideological agenda in relation to Myanmar. Australia was acting largely in concert with the US, the UK, Western Europe, Japan, and the Republic of Korea. But, despite appearances, our sanctions were not closely coordinated or orchestrated: there was no coordinating mechanism whatsoever, no regular meeting, no 'secretariat', and no systematic information sharing (although a great deal of informal consultation and coordination occurred because diplomats are essentially practical people). Nor was there ever any attempt to discuss these sanctions with the Myanmar Government with a view to identifying changes they should make in order to have sanctions lifted. But the (at best) quasi-legal status of international sanctions and their indiscriminate effects — on trade, education, and people's welfare — had a divisive effect inside the country, with most people, except opposition 'true believers', seeming unhappy with sanctions.

The practical effects of Australia's sanctions were not necessarily well understood by Australians dealing with Myanmar, and were not necessarily supported by many of them. The bilateral Australian sanctions, imposed since the 1988 uprising, limited Australian Government support for trade, tourism, investment, and education promotion, and meant that both the quantum and content of Australia's aid program were extremely circumscribed. This meant, for example, that there was no trade or economic officer in the Australian Embassy (only an Austrade local trade officer), no aid program specialist (as there was officially no government-to-government aid), no Australia-based immigration officer (Immigration Department officers from the Australian Embassy in Bangkok visited Yangon periodically to conduct interviews), no education officer, and no defence attaché; it was definitely a second-rank embassy. However, in Australia's case, sanctions were deceptive, because they did not necessarily limit Australia's support for programs carried out by the United Nations, international financial institutions, and other international agencies. However, Australian activists supporting the Burmese democracy movement were strongly in favour of Australia's bilateral sanctions, without necessarily knowing or understanding their full impact — positive or 'negative'. They were, however, prepared to object to Australian scholarships for people from Myanmar, when desperate, even claiming that such scholarships would enable 'the sons and daughters of generals' to study in Australia on Australian Government scholarships.

In the general course of business, the Australian Embassy in Yangon received no instructions or advice or requests from Canberra relating to our sanctions 'regime' against Myanmar. Other than on first encounters — when the absence of Australian aid funding or Australian Government scholarships for study in Australia would normally arise — sanctions would not normally be raised or discussed with senior levels of the military regime. There was really little need for any such discussion more than a decade after these sanctions had been imposed. The Myanmar Government would have assumed that Australian policy would not change in the absence of political change in Myanmar and that in debates at the United Nations, Australia would, as usual, side with the 'West' against Myanmar.

There were only a very limited number of mechanisms whereby sanctions-applying countries with embassies in Yangon met to concert their policies and responses. The main one was the 'mini-Dublin Group' for coordinating counter-narcotics programs, in conjunction with the UNDCP (now the UN Office on Drugs and Crime). Like-minded countries occasionally met in other settings, such as the United Nations, to try to coordinate their approaches to Myanmar and to exchange ideas about how to make more progress, but no such meetings ever occurred in Yangon. Indeed, no such meetings occurred elsewhere between 2000 and 2003, because UN envoys did have satisfactory access to the country at this time, and there were some modest hopes that change might not be far away. Some of these meetings resumed later, at Wilton Park in the UK, for example, but they never produced any significant outcomes, and never had any noticeable influence on the military regime. Australia did not always attend.

However, the background presence of sanctions had the expected negative effect on many aspects of Australia's official and unofficial contacts and interactions with Myanmar: it effectively discouraged Australian tourists, business, and investors, and contributed directly to a gradual decline in almost all manifestations of Australian interest in Myanmar. A few Australians worked in international agencies in Myanmar, but not at senior levels, and from 2000–03 no Australian headed an official international agency in Myanmar. Australians headed — very creditably — a small number of INGOs, such as World Vision, Care International, and World Concern.

Australia benefited enormously from wide appreciation in Myanmar of the well-received work and popular contributions of many individual Australians over many years. Although to this day they are not all recognised in Australia for their roles, they are still remembered by the Myanmar people with whom they worked. Amongst these, for example, were a small number of Australian nuns who were assigned to parts of the Myanmar Catholic Church to carry out educational or community health work. Staff from the Australian Red Cross were occasionally assigned to work with the Myanmar Red Cross Society, sometimes in Yangon, sometimes in regional locations. Some academics based in Australia maintained personal contacts with academic institutions in Myanmar, but some other academics also probably avoided contact with Myanmar.

After about 2000, numerous Australian doctors started coming to Myanmar regularly, often as part of programs whose costs were covered by Rotary Clubs.[1] But the doctors gave their own time *pro bono*, not once but innumerable times, out of their commitment to doing something to help those in need in Myanmar. Their medical programs and activities had no official standing for Australia, but they often were part of official programs of the Myanmar Government. So the Australian Embassy needed to be aware of their activities and be supportive of them. Occasionally, the embassy helped with any administrative problems, but more often they were well organised and well prepared for what they wanted to do. How sustainable all this was is debatable, but a strong component of all the programs was exposure for Myanmar doctors and nurses and additional skills training in Australia. The key Myanmar organisation was the Myanmar Medical Association (MMA) — a group composed of senior Myanmar medical practitioners who were still active in their (essentially government-controlled) profession. The MMA's leaders' understanding of their role was impressive, their professional skills substantial, and their commitment to high medical principles formidable.

Only a small number of Australians were present in the international community in Yangon, but whether working for humanitarian NGOs or as small business people, all were highly regarded, and were known for their effectiveness, outgoing natures, and their empathy with ordinary Burmese. The Australian Red Cross, for example, quite often provided expert staff to the Myanmar Red Cross Society and the International Committee of the Red Cross, one of only four Red Cross societies in the world providing such in-country support. At this time, no problems emanating from the local Australian community ever brought Australia into disrepute. The fact that some INGOs such as World Vision, Care Myanmar, and later Marie Stopes International were run from Australia, and were usually managed by Australians as Country Director, also enhanced Australia's local standing.

---

1   These groups included Interplast (cleft palate surgery); cardiac experts under Dr Alan Gale from the Adventist Hospital in Sydney; eye surgery teams under Dr James Muecke from Adelaide Hospital; Professor Bruce Conolly from the Sydney Hospital Hand Surgery Unit; Professor Bob Bauze from Adelaide University; and Professor Alan Pearson from the Nursing School of Adelaide University.

Another Australian 'asset' was the *Myanmar Times*, which had begun operations in 2000 as a joint venture with military intelligence without the benefit of a broader strategic plan. Under the direction of a hard drinking, hard-living 'rogue' of an Australian journalist, Ross Dunkley, the *Myanmar Times* sought in its own way to change Myanmar Government policy, worked diligently to reveal aspects of Myanmar and its people that were not normally covered in government-controlled media, and eventually endeavoured to interpret developments in Myanmar sensitively and objectively to the international community. It also went out of its way to publicise — very helpfully — Australian policies and initiatives towards Myanmar, so that Australia achieved a considerably higher profile than it otherwise would have had. At any time, several Australian journalists worked on the staff of the newspaper, as writers, trainers, and in senior managerial positions. Not long after it started, the *Myanmar Times* began providing significant training programs for its Myanmar journalists.[2]

The *Myanmar Times* was a joint business venture (Myanmar Consolidated Media) between Western Australian newspapers — and Bill Clough in particular — and a Myanmar businessman connected to military intelligence. Ross Dunkley was widely criticised in 'activist' circles for agreeing to work under strict censorship of a regime that activists regarded as illegitimate. The life and work of Ross Dunkley and the *Myanmar Times* was later featured in the interesting 2011 documentary film, *Dancing with Dictators: The Story of the Last Foreign Publisher in Burma*. Dunkley was sometimes accused of acting as 'an apologist' for the regime, and lacking independence and integrity, but the *Myanmar Times* was always run transparently and was prepared to publish articles critical of the military regime when it could. Dunkley was personally openly opposed to many regime policies and showed courage in challenging regime policies in

---

2   According to Wikipedia: 'Myanmar Consolidated Media is the largest private media company in Myanmar and employs more than 300 staff and has bureaus in Mandalay and Naypyitaw. The paper has a circulation of around 25,000 copies in Burmese and 3,000 copies in English. A January 2008 report said the Burmese edition is the country's largest circulation newspaper, while the English edition is the only privately owned and operated English-language newspaper in the country.' See en.wikipedia.org/wiki/The_Myanmar_Times.

the early 2000s, although this happened very rarely. Dunkley later achieved international prominence when he had a falling out with the regime and was arrested in 2011.[3]

There was also a handful of smaller Australian businessmen living and working in Myanmar on a long-term basis who appeared to be respected and recognised in the local community. Larger Australian firms such as Broken Hill Propriety Limited, which would normally play a leading role in the foreign business community in Southeast Asia, had closed their office in 1995 after waiting in vain for more open economic policies to deliver suitable commercial opportunities. The smaller Australian entrepreneurs often ran small, even one-person companies in somewhat specialised areas with valuable technical skills such as environmental equipment, mining and energy services, interior decorating, and legal services. They sourced goods and services from Australia, contributing to the very modest bilateral trade volume. A few other Australians were working as individuals in the hospitality, tourism, and education sectors. Given the small size of the international community overall, some of these Australians occasionally had a quite a high profile in the local community and were sometimes well known to prominent Myanmar leaders.

As a general impression, Australians residing in Myanmar at this time tended not to be taking inappropriate advantage of military rule in Myanmar. Indeed, many of them were participating in humanitarian and welfare activities, including through Christian organisations. If any Australians were involved in any kind of dubious or illicit activities, these tended not to come to light. With an Australian Federal Police presence in the Australian Embassy after 2000 producing good working relationships with the Myanmar law enforcement authorities, it could be anticipated that untoward Australian activities would come to notice, as happened elsewhere. By and large, during this period — due in large part to the very low number of Australian tourists travelling to Myanmar — the Australian Embassy experienced very few significant consular problems.

---

3   Some aspects of Dunkley's work in Myanmar were described by Chris Maldon after Dunkley was imprisoned on apparently trumped-up charges, on which he was found guilty but was eventually freed. See 'Newspaper Boss Ross Dunkley to Renew Push for Free Media in Burma', *The Australian*, 2 July 2011. Available at www.theaustralian.com.au/news/world/newspaper-boss-ross-dunkley-to-renew-push-for-free-media-in-burma/story-e6frg6so-1226085874701.

At the same time, there were very few Australian tourists or private citizens visiting Myanmar. This was quite an abnormal situation, especially when compared with the numbers visiting Thailand next door. Although Australian pro-democracy advocates did not formally seek to ban tourism, some Australian sympathisers, such as the trade union movement and some of the small political parties, did call for a ban on tourism, but without success. A few small Australian travel companies continued to promote tourism to Myanmar, at least until 2003; after the 30 May 2003 attack on Aung San Suu Kyi at Depayin, companies such as Intrepid stopped dealing with Myanmar, and did not resume operations there until after 2010. Australian Government policy at this time was not to intervene against normal commercial activities. Daw Aung San Suu Kyi's support for a tourism boycott was sometimes stated vigorously, but her position changed to one of tolerating individual tourism, but not mass tourism, for which Myanmar Government assistance might be required. To my knowledge, Australian tourists and tourism companies were not directly involved in supporting Myanmar Government activity. The NLD never drew our attention to inappropriate activities by Australian travel companies.

One of the very few high-profile consular 'cases' involving Australian travellers in this period was that of the human rights activist James Mawdsley, a British–Australian dual citizen who was imprisoned in Kengtung prison in eastern Shan State in 1999, and who was, by agreement, receiving consular assistance from the British Embassy. As Wikipedia explains, Mawdsley is

> a Catholic seminarian who is also a human rights activist campaigning for democracy in Burma. He is a dual citizen of the United Kingdom and Australia. He was born in 1972. He gave up his studying at Bristol University to teach English at a Burmese refugee camp. Mawdsley was arrested three times for his involvement and deported three times. He spent over a year in a prison in Myanmar during 1999 and 2000 and was also tortured, as part of a seventeen-year jail sentence, after taking part in pro-democracy protests in Rangoon.

Mawdsley had let it be known that he wanted to be arrested again by the Myanmar authorities, and it appears that he was writing a diary of his imprisonment for later publication. The Australian Embassy kept itself informed about Mawdsley's situation through the British Embassy during the year of his imprisonment. I met his (Australian) mother when she came to visit him in late 2000, but only met

Mawdsley himself at Yangon airport after his release from Kengtung prison when he was being deported to the UK. Mawdsley's book detailing his campaign against the military regime's human rights abuses acknowledges the efforts of my predecessor, Lyndall McLean, on his behalf.[4]

Other Australians who left a distinctive mark inside and outside Myanmar at this time were a small number of Australian academic experts on Myanmar undertaking research in-country and publishing it in high-quality, world-renowned publications. Several of these scholars were social scientists connected with The Australian National University: Helen James, an expert on education and civil society in Myanmar; Andrew Selth, an expert on the Myanmar military who was later affiliated with Griffith University near Brisbane; anthropologist Monique Skidmore, author of *Karaoke Fascism*; and the Danish-born, Canberra-based PhD scholar and later political scientist, Morten Pedersen.[5] Other scholars working out of Australia, and undertaking notable research in Myanmar at this time included Sean Turnell at Macquarie University in Sydney, and anthropologist Nancy Hudson-Rodd at Edith Cowan University in Perth. All these scholars were successful in undertaking significant research on quite sensitive topics in Myanmar at this time.

Another type of Australian visitor — often probably visiting without the knowledge of the Australian Government — was the occasional academic visiting Myanmar for personal/professional research, or as a *'pro bono'* action helping Burmese universities with advanced courses or postgraduate supervision. Sometimes members of Australian churches visited in a missionary-like role, although more often to perform social work for their Myanmar counterpart church than to engage in religious proselytising. These highly dedicated people usually had little or no contact with the Australian Embassy, although I met a few occasionally at the embassy or social gatherings. I discovered that whatever activities these people were engaged in,

---

4   James Mawdsley's book, *The Iron Road: A Stand for Truth and Democracy in Burma,* New York: North Point Press, 2001, was published not long after his release.

5   Andrew Selth published *Burma's Armed Forces: Power Without Glory* in 2002; Monique Skidmore published *Karaoke Fascism: Burma and the Politics of Fear* in 2004; Helen James published *Security and Sustainable Development in Myanmar* in 2006; and Morten Pedersen published *Promoting Human Rights in Burma: A Critique of Western Sanctions Policy* in 2008. They were all carrying out in-country research between 2000–03.

their contributions were enormously appreciated by the Burmese people they were working with. (Australia was far from alone in having such 'humanitarian volunteers' spending time in Myanmar, in contrast to the isolation and sanctions practised under government policies. There were many more people from the US and the UK.)

Some Australians with a strong interest in Burma avoided visiting Burma under the military regime; some, especially those with connections to the activist movement, preferred to work with the large and relatively settled Burmese refugees on the Thai–Burma border. There were a few exceptions to this. One individual with overt political connections who did visit Burma, despite being on the military regime's visa 'black list',[6] was the New South Wales Labor party politician Janelle Saffin, who had quite extensive connections with the National League for Democracy. Janelle Saffin was one of a very small number of people at this time who recognised that political change in Myanmar might be getting nearer. She was later (in 2007) to become a Labor member of the federal parliament, an advisor to Labor prime ministers Rudd and Gillard, and — after the transition to the Thein Sein Government — a tireless campaigner for rebuilding the full range of Australian relations with Myanmar. I recall telling staff in the Myanmar Ministry of Foreign Affairs and the Myanmar Embassy in Canberra at the time — not acting on any official instructions — that it was not in their interests to ban Australian academics from visiting Myanmar, no matter what they said or wrote, and mentioning Janelle Saffin by name as an example.

The period between 2000–03 saw a number of Australians coming to Myanmar as 'good Samaritans', trying to help the ordinary people of Myanmar in one way or another. My predecessor as ambassador, Lyndall McLean, and her husband even came into this category when they returned in 2002 to work for a UN agency and a private company respectively. Another category of visitors was project managers from various Australian Rotary Clubs[7] undertaking humanitarian projects — their projects ranging from building water supplies to the provision of medical equipment and medical services and training — although

---

6   Janelle Saffin's visa applications around this period were mostly unsuccessful because of this, but on at least one occasion she managed to obtain a tourist visa in Bangkok and called on the Australian Embassy in Yangon.

7   These included Rotary Clubs from New South Wales, Victoria, Western Australia, and the Australian Capital Territory, but there could have been more.

they rarely had any direct requirements of the embassy. Their activities were all carried out with the knowledge and approval of the Myanmar authorities, often through the intermediation of the Myanmar Medical Association — and often with the direct approval of the Myanmar customs authorities — and never in this period caused problems for the Australian Embassy or the Australian Government. Indeed, the embassy enjoyed very good relations with the Myanmar Medical Association, which in later years also sponsored high-level Myanmar medical delegations to Australia.

As a measure of their commitment to assisting Myanmar, a number of these Australian individuals subsequently established their own charitable NGOs (or non-profit organisations (NPOs)) to cover their ongoing operations in Myanmar. These organisations include Sight for All, based in Adelaide, and the Conolly Medical Foundation for Myanmar, based in Sydney. Possibly the most successful Australian NGO to be set up in this period is Graceworks Myanmar, set up by retired Australian businessman Peter Simmons in Melbourne, which was able to operate effectively with a range of local partners in a variety of humanitarian and capacity-building fields in and around Yangon, with the approval of the Myanmar authorities, and largely without interference from them. Their activities were carried out in the public eye, and often attracted publicity — in Myanmar and/or in Australia — but this was usually low-key, modest publicity that offended nobody, but definitely helped fundraising. Some of these activities also received partial funding from the Australian aid program.

The activities of these individuals and groups were uniquely Australian. They were not the product of consultation with other countries, they were not part of broader programs that were regional or global in their character, they were not even 'blessed' by elements of the United Nations, and they were not the result of any ingenious Australian Government strategy to influence and change Myanmar. But they were all conducted openly and transparently and in accordance with accepted 'best practice'. They all achieved identifiable results, were 'sustainable', and mostly continued for several years and gradually expanded the range of their activities. The individuals involved brought credit to Australia through their undertakings. They also brought many more Australians into some form of contact with Myanmar, including as visitors.

Australian media visitors, however, were few and far between. They were usually based in Bangkok, as were the ABC correspondents, and visited Yangon only from time to time to report, mostly when significant events were happening. Often they could not obtain a journalist visa, which was a problem; occasionally, I was asked to intercede with the Myanmar authorities to assist their visa applications, which I normally did. A few other Australian journalists visited, but not many. As Australian Ambassador, I often received requests for interviews with visiting Western journalists such as the *Financial Times* (and sometimes Japanese journalists), which at that time I could agree to do without consultation with Canberra. Some of these media visitors had also been in contact with my predecessors. I felt it was worth responding to such requests, as Western media access was on the whole so limited, and anything to expand the information available was beneficial. I don't recall any embarrassing consequences from this at all, and did not feel pressured to promote any particular political 'line' as long as I was providing factual information about developments or Australian policy.

Very few Australian politicians visited Myanmar during these years, largely because visiting under a military regime might have implied some kind of endorsement of the status quo, or because it might have required some overt criticism of the regime, which might or might not have been appropriate. It was unusual for an Australian embassy not to have to look after a stream of Australian political visitors, but the absence of a parliament in Myanmar actually meant this lack of visitors was logical and unsurprising. There were few political visitors from other countries (with perhaps the exception of Japan), so Australia did not stand out. In other words, it was highly unlikely that political visitors to Myanmar at such an uncertain and polarised time would have achieved anything. Alexander Downer's visit to Yangon in early October 2002 occurred just before the Bali bombing on 12 October 2002, an event which significantly distracted political attention from issues other than terrorism for some time. Over the next year or so, no questions were asked about Burma in the Australian Parliament, in contrast with earlier periods. Nor did many Australian officials visit Myanmar during this period: with a wide range of activities sanctioned, there was little practical work for Australian officials to pursue. In the early 2000s, when some smaller Australian universities began to look further afield for international students —

or even possible sites for off-shore campuses — and started making exploratory visits to Myanmar, we saw a few Australian academic entrepreneurs coming through, but they faced many practical obstacles and considerable competition from other countries, so it took some time before their plans materialised.[8]

One international institution which had taken root in Yangon some years before my arrival was the Hash House Harriers, the running and walking club, mainly for foreigners, which had its origins in British colonial times in Kuala Lumpur.[9] Participating regularly in the weekly Yangon 'Hash' was, for me, an invaluable way of seeing parts of the city the authorities did not normally want foreigners to enter — as a result, the Hash House Harriers event often attracted the attention of the security authorities. Participating also brought a great range of people from different countries and different jobs into contact, but in an informal and friendly ambience. I occasionally invited other ambassadorial colleagues to participate, which they found most interesting, but perhaps not commensurate with their status. It was also a place where many locally based or visiting Australians would gather. Overall, the Hash House Harriers provided opportunities for anyone participating in the run/walk to ascertain how the Myanmar interests of residents and visitors in very different occupations were faring, and what unannounced initiatives were under way. But there were also a few Burmese men and women who participated very wholeheartedly in the activities, and were always interesting to talk with. Many short-term visitors, including quite a few from Australia, would find their way to the Yangon Hash House Harriers each week.

The Hash House Harriers was where I learnt more about how the Myanmar authorities were 'managing' their 2002–03 bank crisis than would ever come out through the media or scholarly writings.[10] I was fortunate enough to befriend a fellow walker who was a consultant for the Yoma Bank, one of the private Myanmar banks caught up in the run on the banks that occurred. (Unrelated to the crisis, Yoma Bank

---

8   Educators from Australia at this time included some from Curtin University in Western Australia and the University of Central Queensland in Rockhampton.

9   See the Wikipedia entry at en.wikipedia.org/wiki/Hash_House_Harriers.

10   The Australian economist who specialises in Myanmar, Professor Sean Turnell from Macquarie University in Sydney, wrote the most detailed account in his *Fiery Dragons: Banks, Moneylenders and Microfinance in Burma,* Copenhagen: NIAS Press, 2009. However, Turnell was not in Myanmar during the crisis.

was trying to install modern electronic banking systems for the first time across its branches in Myanmar.) What was known in banking circles was that when the bank crisis was at its most serious point — probably during February and March 2003 — the Myanmar Government was convening a daily meeting of the main banks and the government representatives, led by the Ministry of Finance and the Central Bank of Myanmar, but also including military intelligence. The purpose was to monitor closely the demands on the private banks, and to manage and direct their responses, to avoid the situation worsening and getting out of control. While my walking 'friend' was fairly careful in what he disclosed, he indicated that questions about how to manage deposits at the customer level and the banks' capitalisation were on the table.

Unsurprisingly, some of the decisions taken by the Myanmar authorities left the banks uncomfortable, and the regulators were fairly authoritarian in their approach, but the overall process was more inclusive than might have been expected, and was certainly very 'hands-on'. Reassuring Myanmar consumers — no easy task, given that they had always been notoriously sceptical about banks — was a high priority. Thus, on 21 February 2003, the head of the government, Secretary One General Khin Nyunt, issued a statement announcing a Central Bank loan to the private banks in question (including Yoma Bank) and seeking to reassure people that private banks were safe.[11] Details of what was going on behind the scenes were not secret, but for obvious reasons were not being advertised. Subsequently, private depositors and local businesses lost quite substantial amounts, but the banking system — such as it was — survived. (Yoma Bank, never very close to the government, was criticised for unspecified breaches of its obligations, but continues operating and today remains the second largest private bank in Myanmar.)

The weekly Hash House Harriers event often meant going to parts of Yangon where the authorities might prefer foreigners not to go: areas where there was extreme poverty; areas where local residents were openly less supportive of the authorities; and areas where the Myanmar authorities' presence was, for one reason or another, problematical — there might be an 'off-limits' military establishment, military activities

---

11   This was reported on page one of the *Myanmar Times* of 24 February in an article entitled 'S1 reassures public that private banks are safe'.

that were not for public acknowledgement, or questionable police behaviour. So the Hash House Harriers group occasionally found itself at odds with the security authorities, but since it was officially acceptable to move around anywhere in Yangon, there was little the local police could do about this. (In practice, the Hash group went out of its way to respect local practices — removing footwear if we passed through a monastery, for example.) On one occasion, as the local security agent tried surreptitiously to photograph Hash participants, we turned the tables by asking him to take a group photograph of the Hash with his own camera. On another occasion, the Australian Federal Police representative from the Australian Embassy was acting as the 'hare', setting the trail for the Hash running event, but was arrested for trespassing near a military camp. He was released by the police when they discovered his identity, but the Hash proceeded to have an illustrated t-shirt printed to commemorate that occasion.

Eventually, I was given the 'Hash name' of 'Ambolator', appropriate since I always walked rather than ran, and much more respectable than some of the names other participants were given. After my return to Australian and my retirement, while working on Myanmar at The Australian National University, I would endeavour to join up with the Yangon Hash House Harriers whenever I visited Myanmar. It was still an enjoyable and relaxing institution where one could understand a different side of Myanmar.

10

Early Australian Public Diplomacy Possible in Myanmar

Engaging in public diplomacy in another country necessarily involves judgments about mutual benefits arising from exposing the people of another country to the intellectual achievements or artistic accomplishments of the 'giving' country, weighed against the possibility of undertaking an activity that might be inappropriate, sensitive, or even offensive in terms of the culture of the 'receiving' country. Occasionally, it can mean promoting the values of systems that are opposed to those of the recipient country (as in the Soviet Union, for example). In post-2000 Yangon, several foreign governments sought to engage in 'traditional' public diplomacy: the highly organised and well-funded operations of the former US Information Agency and the British Council were the leading exponents of such programs, pursuing both sides of the template. But even less well-funded programs, from countries such as Japan, France, and others, increased their activity in this area post-2000 as it seemed that full-scale political transformation was still some time away, while a modest but encouraging degree of 'opening up' was under way under the otherwise authoritarian military regime. The nature of other countries' public diplomacy varied: Japan tended to prefer film festivals, which could be conducted as a commercial activity but targeted a wide community, and presumably went through normal censorship; some countries chose to organise 'in house' activities such as music recitals, which were not aimed at the wider Burmese community, and therefore would not attract interference from the authorities; the British and the Americans gradually increased their English teaching activities, which covertly targeted political opposition members, but did not have an overt political purpose.

By its very nature, public diplomacy was an area where the embassy would run up against the regime's controls on freedom of expression. Any material that was published for public consumption, whether printed word or images, had to pass censorship controls; any public event not held within the confines of the embassy required permission from the authorities. These were not untried waters: other embassies and organisations had undertaken similar activities, or had to obtain official permission to carry out their public activities. But they obviously presented policy and organisational challenges, and there was a degree of unpredictability about the outcome. Potentially, the possibility of adverse media or negative public impact was greater than in a non-authoritarian environment.

When I arrived in Yangon in May 2000, the Australian Government was not really prepared for a shift away from its hitherto extremely low-profile range of activities. As a low-rated embassy in terms of its size and the cool political relationship with Myanmar, the Australian Embassy in Yangon generally did not figure in Canberra's plans or budgeting for public diplomacy activity. Indeed, before 2000 the embassy was not allocated any public diplomacy funds by DFAT. Realistically, there was not a lot of global or generic public diplomacy activity that would have been suitable for Myanmar. The embassy was mostly left to its own devices about what it wished to do, subject to informing DFAT in Canberra in advance (usually by simply including any proposed activity in the embassy's annual public diplomacy plan). Sometimes embassy 'support' might be no more than the ambassador offering to host an event at the embassy, using official entertainment allowance funds. Yet, some other countries that imposed sanctions had begun modest public diplomacy programs. So it was apparent that, even in a highly controlled environment such as Myanmar in the early 2000s, it would be possible to project a distinct, but genuine, Australian profile and to work with various stakeholders or proponents, while conforming with broader Australian Government directions and standards to maintain the integrity of the events or activities.

The Australian Embassy's limited experience with only a small number of lesser public diplomacy activities in the challenging but changing political environment of 2000–03 confirmed that the military regime's tentative signs of opening up could be translated into embassies carrying out more 'normal' diplomatic activities in Yangon, including public diplomacy events, despite the restrictions that applied on political activity, freedom of expression, and 'fraternisation' with ordinary Burmese people. This was contrary to many preconceptions that existed in Australia and the West, but was consistent with the experience of many other embassies in Yangon at that time.

Given the extremely modest resources available, it was very much a matter of 'making the best out of very little'. An effective way to promote Australian food and wine was at the annual Australia Day reception, where we were able to take advantage of the existing efficient 'supply chain' links from Australian suppliers to supermarkets, restaurants, and hotels in Myanmar, enabling us to organise impressive Australia-sourced catering for the reception at the Australian Club.

In addition, a few significant Australian occasions or events were marked by the Australian Embassy in Yangon between 2000 and 2003. In a variety of ways, these events inevitably involved some interaction with the military regime and its policies and practices, beyond what would be the case in countries without an authoritarian government. The main objective was to carry out these events in the way the Australian parties preferred; the main challenge was to judge how to go forward if the Myanmar authorities decided to amend or adjust the character of the event. The ultimate test was to assess whether or not it had been possible to preserve the 'integrity' of the event, and whether or not holding it had been worthwhile and meant achieving some progress for the Burmese people affected.

These events included the Sydney Olympic Games, the 50th anniversary of the Qantas Kangaroo Route, the 50th anniversary of Australia–Burma diplomatic relations and the 60th anniversary of the Burma–Thailand Railway.

Australia Day

Events to mark Australia's national day are a high point in Australia's public diplomacy around the world, and it was little different in Yangon from 2000 to 2003, although local circumstances influenced the style and nature of the event. As in other countries, the Australian Embassy in Yangon sought to bring members of the Australian community together with local people, who were cooperating with Australia to celebrate Australian connections with Myanmar, with special Australian food and wine, and sometimes musical performances. The end of January is the coolest time of the year in Myanmar, with minimum temperatures around 19 degrees Celsius and maximums around 30 degrees Celsius, with almost no possibility of rain, so a wet weather plan was never needed. The setting for the Australia Day reception was the outdoor area of Australian Club within the grounds of the ambassador's residence, with special lighting for the occasion.

In Yangon by this time, the advent of Australian professionals in the hospitality sector and the arrival of quality Australia food products in the up-market City Mart supermarket chain in Yangon made it possible to stage quite an impressive Australia Day function at the ambassador's residence. Each year we sought to showcase something different and exotic in the way of Australian food, sharing the day with the Indian Embassy, whose national day falls on the same day. (Alcohol was not normally served at the Indian national day reception, so local practice was for invitees to attend the Indian receptions first and then proceed to the Australian reception.) In the early 2000s, Australian embassies across the world received a special budget allocation for the Australia Day reception, based on a plan submitted by each embassy in advance. This enabled the Yangon Embassy to put the catering arrangements for the reception out to competitive tender from a few of Yangon's better hotels. We had a small organising committee within the embassy, which included myself and my wife, who had considerable experience of such events from our times in Tokyo.

In Yangon in the early 2000s, while aiming to welcome a suitably high-level government representative — usually the foreign minister — senior representatives of the NLD also normally attended, although the two would not necessarily speak to one another. At this time, there were not many events at which both government representatives and NLD representatives were present. The NLD was generally represented at Australia Day by Deputy Chairman Tin Oo, although the Chairman, U Aung Shwe, as a former Ambassador to Australia, would also attend, health permitting. (Aung San Suu Kyi did not attend, as this was not permitted by the Myanmar authorities until much later.) Another former Myanmar Ambassador to Australia who regularly attended our reception was Brigadier Maung Maung,[1] who was the long retired architect of the modern Burmese Army and who had been a key figure in the 'Caretaker Government' of 1958–60 under General Ne Win. While the military regime did not interfere overtly with the event, some government officials inevitably felt that they should not attend. But a reasonable cross-section of Yangon society mostly did attend. We never felt constrained in who we invited, or what we did at the event. Since we had no formal military-to-military relationship, we did not invite members of the Myanmar military, and so did not have numbers of Burmese in military uniform present. (A representative of the Australian Defence Attaché's Office from Bangkok who was accredited to Myanmar usually attended, but the senior defence attaché was normally required to attend the equivalent event in Bangkok.)

The social columns of the Australian-run *Myanmar Times* provided coverage of the embassy's Australia Day event for their own purposes.

Sydney Olympic Games 2000

Myanmar is a member of the Olympic movement and sent a small team of seven athletes to the Sydney Olympic Games in September 2000. As a matter of course, we invited the Myanmar team to a farewell party at the ambassador's residence. The games were also an opportunity to celebrate Australia's achievements. In this case, our embassy obviously had the benefit of a wealth of marketing and publicity material generated by the Sydney Olympics Committee and the federal and NSW state governments. One interesting aspect of this for

---

1   Brigadier Maung Maung paid a courtesy call on me at the embassy after my arrival in Yangon, which was exactly that — a courtesy call. Brigadier Maung Maung was quite elderly by this time, but he remained in reasonable health, while being somewhat eccentric. His two daughters had stayed on in Australia and were Australian citizens married to Australians. They returned to Yangon from time to time to keep in touch with their family.

Myanmar was the case of the Sports Minister, Brigadier-General Aye Myint, being allowed to attend in spite of Australian travel bans on members of the Myanmar military regime. (Aye Myint resigned from the army to stand for election for the government Union Social and Development Party in November 2010, and was appointed Minister of Science and Technology in President Thein Sein's first cabinet in 2011, before being appointed Minister of Industry in 2012, and then Minister of Labour, Employment and Social Security in 2014.)[2]

Fiftieth anniversary of Qantas's Kangaroo Route, 2001

Whose idea was it to celebrate the 50th anniversary of Qantas's Kangaroo Route from London to Sydney by staging an air race of small planes in 2002 over the route? An assortment of more than 40 aircrafts from all over the world left the UK on 11 March 2001 at the start of a 22,000 km journey to Australia, stopping at many countries that became well-known stopover points on the original 'Kangaroo Route' between England and Australia. Stopover and transit points included France, Greece, Crete, Egypt, Saudi Arabia, Bahrain, United Arab Emirates, Oman, Pakistan, India, Myanmar, Thailand, Singapore, Indonesia, and Timor, finally making their first Australian landfall at Darwin. The 'Kangaroo Route' originally included Yangon, but it was a very long time since Qantas had stopped over regularly in Yangon.

The Myanmar Government gave all-out support for this event, presumably conscious that its handling of the stopover in Yangon would be compared with others along the route, and also presumably also because it saw the air race as a recognition of Myanmar's rightful place. They would also have calculated that a successful (accident-free) stopover, even if only 12 hours in duration, could generate considerable positive publicity. Most of the arrangements for the stopover were handled by the air race organisers directly with the Myanmar civil aviation authorities. The Australian Embassy was primarily involved in the 'hospitality' arrangements for the pilots at the Inya Lake Hotel. However, the extent of the Myanmar Government's

---

2   According to ALTSEAN's Regime Watch. See www.altsean.org/Research/Regime%20Watch/Executive/Cabinet.php.

supporting arrangement were unexpected: Deputy Minister for Transport Brigadier-General Kyaw Myint was stationed in the air traffic control tower overseeing aircraft landing activity for most of the time; Foreign Minister U Win Aung and Transport Minister Hla Myint Swe, a higher ranking general, greeted the aircraft on arrival; and the government newspaper, the *New Light of Myanmar*, carried a prominent factual story on the stopover the following day.[3]

The stopover at Yangon was accomplished safely and successfully, and without incident. Despite fears that the crossing of the Bay of Bengal involved risks for such small planes with minimal navigation systems, no casualties occurred during the transit of Myanmar, and no consular problems arose from the participants for the Australian Embassy in Yangon. The Myanmar Government's support, neither solicited nor anticipated, contributed considerably to this outcome. But embassy staff had to invest a great deal of time and effort into the exercise, and were gratified by the satisfactory outcome. It was not clear whether the larrikin actions of some of the pilots — landing on beaches, roads, etc. — were known to the authorities at the time. But if they did know about these relatively harmless incidents through their normal military intelligence networks, they were politely tight-lipped.

The air race certainly gained great publicity for Australia, although the Myanmar transit, among so many stopovers during the race, was probably not a stand-out event. Quite a lot of responsibility was carried by the Australian diplomatic posts involved, but whether this was fully appreciated by the organisers or by the Australian Government is not certain. It was written up enthusiastically by the *Myanmar Times* more than once.

Fiftieth anniversary of Australia–Burma diplomatic relations, 2002

In May 1952, an Australian diplomatic office was opened in Yangon for the first time, just over three years after Burma gained its independence, and Australia's relationships with Burma began.

---

3   See 'Yangon Landing for Air Race', *New Light of Myanmar,* 13 November 2000; and 'Aircraft in Sydney Air Race 2001 Stop Over at Yangon International Airport', *New Light of Myanmar,* 27 March 2001.

The fiftieth anniversary of diplomatic relations was thus marked in May 2002. DFAT would normally mark significant anniversaries of bilateral relations in some way or other, such as when the fiftieth anniversary of the establishment of diplomatic relations was reached, but relations with Burma (now Myanmar) in 2002 under a 'despised' military regime was not an appropriate cause for lavish celebration. I do not recall receiving any instructions from Canberra in connection with this anniversary.[4]

In the embassy, however, we did do the bare minimum, feeling that it was inappropriate to ignore the occasion altogether. Vice Minister of Foreign Affairs U Khin Maung Win kindly agreed to be guest of honour at a small reception in the embassy, which also marked the refurbishment of the embassy. Having been in the same fairly prestigious location next to the Strand Hotel for most of the period, but having just recently been refurbished — even if on a very modest scale — the Australian Embassy was a widely recognised presence. The Australian-owned and managed *Myanmar Times* loyally reported the event on its front page. My recollection is that the very brief report we sent to DFAT on the event drew little or no response from Canberra.

Sixtieth anniversary of the Burma–Thailand Railway, 2003

A more moving event was the special service the Australian Embassy organised for the World War II prisoners of war who returned to Myanmar on the occasion of the 60th anniversary of the Burma–Thailand Railway in May 2003. As this trip was not an officially supported event, it was entirely organised through private channels, with little or no involvement from the Department of Veterans' Affairs.[5] The Burma terminus of the railway, Thanbyuzayat, has been accessible for many years, but until recently it had not been possible for visitors

---

4   Perhaps reflecting the extent Australia's diplomatic history is coloured by the Commonwealth and the Cold War, Burma also receives only the briefest of mentions in the official departmental history of Australian engagement with Asia, *Facing North*. The only references are in Peter Gifford's chapter 'The Cold War Across Asia', in Goldsworthy, David (ed.), *Facing North: A Century of Australian Engagement with Asia*, Melbourne: Melbourne University Press, 2001, pp. 172, 175.
5   In the words of the Minister for Veteran Affairs, in another context, Burma 'is not a country with which the Department has any dealings'. Letter from Minister for Veterans' Affairs Dana Vale to Trevor Wilson, 11 September 2003.

to travel even a short distance down the WWII railway track, because of clashes that occurred as part of the continuing insurgency in the area. As in Thailand, the WWII railway track had been taken up, and the only signs of it are the trackbeds, embankments, and some bridges. Although only around 200 km by road from the capital Yangon, travel to Thanbyuzayat is not easy. Nowadays, foreign visitors to the railway usually hire a vehicle (mini-bus or four-wheel drive) in Yangon for the trip to Thanbyuzayat, a drive of at least eight hours, quite a tiring journey for the elderly former POWs.[6] Construction of a new bridge across the Salween River (and extension of the railway line from Yangon) to Mawlamyaing in 2004 made the trip shorter and slightly more comfortable.

Through communication with the Australian organisers of the POWs' pilgrimage many months ahead of the visit, the Australian Embassy in Yangon organised a special tribute to the POWs in the form of a special service at the Commonwealth War Cemetery at Thanbyuzayat on 1 May 2003.[7] Several of the POWs were returning to Burma for the first time since their imprisonment, including Dr Rowley Richards, by then 82 years old and a remarkably dignified and disciplined figure.[8] Representatives of Myanmar groups showed their respect by attending, including the military regime's 'mayor' of Thanbyuzayat, the retired professor of history from Mawlamyaing University, and representatives from other POW country embassies (US, UK, and the Netherlands, but not Japan or Thailand). A representative from the opposition New Mon State Party was probably present as well. A Burmese Anglican priest from Mawlamyaing, Rev. Sonny Movin, conducted the religious aspects of the service. For local Myanmar people, it was quite a moving occasion, as their own remembering of this history has not been very consistent or open, and it is still not known how many Burmese labourers died on the railway.

---

6   See Michelle Gorman's article 'Travelling a Track of Sad Memories', *Myanmar Times*, 24 December 2001 – 6 January 2002, Vol. 5, No. 95–96.

7   The Australian Embassy did not seek SPDC approval to hold this event, but out of courtesy notified the Foreign Ministry of our intentions, not expecting any problems as ANZAC Day and Remembrance Day (11 November) were already celebrated annually.

8   His personal account of his wartime experiences was published soon after this anniversary as *A Doctor's War*, Sydney: Harper-Collins, 2005.

In Australia, this particular anniversary was not marked by any significant events or initiatives.[9] The Department of Veterans' Affairs published a memorial monograph to mark the 60th anniversary, *Australians on the Burma–Thailand Railway*.[10] However, in mid-2002 no official messages from Australia were received — or needed. At this time, prisoners of war generally did not get much recognition in the Australian Government's war commemoration activities, so no official activity was planned to mark the 60th anniversary of the railway. More attention might have been accorded the occasion in Thailand, which was much more accessible and had developed good facilities to celebrate the famous railway project. The ceremony at the Thanbyuzayat cemetery in May 2003 was very positively written up in the Australian prisoner of war magazine, *Barbed Wire and Bamboo*.[11]

In subsequent years, in Australia, Myanmar, and Japan, greater attention was focused on the Burma–Thailand Railway prisoner of war experiences.[12]

Generic public diplomacy challenges (or opportunities)

Kunwinjku Aboriginal art exhibition

The one notable exception in regular public diplomacy was a relatively small but stunning exhibition of Arnhem Land Aboriginal art, *Seasons of the Kunwinjku*, which the Department of Foreign Affairs and Trade curated and was taking around Asia and Africa. The Australian Embassy in Yangon arranged for the paintings from West Arnhem Land to be exhibited in the Sedona Hotel in Yangon in 2002. The SPDC

---

9   The Department of Veterans' Affairs in Canberra did maintain a website on the anniversary. See trove.nla.gov.au/work/29881891?selectedversion=NBD44466515.

10   John Moreman, *Australians on the Burma–Thailand Railway 1942–43*, Canberra: Department of Veterans' Affairs, 2003.

11   An account of their trip, written from the perspective of POWs, and authored by Terry Beaton, was published as 'Burma Remembered: An Incredible Experience' in the July/August 2003 issue of *Barbed Wire and Bamboo*.

12   The Australian War Memorial subsequently created a special website in association with a POW exhibition. See www.awm.gov.au/exhibitions/stolenyears/ww2/japan/burmathai/. In 2005, Palgrave Macmillan published *Railwaymen in the War: Tales by Japanese Railway Soldiers in Burma*, by Kazuo Tamayama, the first Japanese account in English.

Deputy Minister for Culture, U Soe Nyunt, a famous poet and writer, and one of the few civilians in Myanmar's Cabinet, kindly opened the exhibition for us.

The 'official' description of the paintings probably does justice to them.

> Australia's Department of Foreign Affairs and Trade is proud to present the art exhibition 'Seasons of the Kunwinjku' by artists from the Kunwinjku clans of West Arnhem Land, Northern Territory. This collection of contemporary Indigenous Australian art reflects the stylistic techniques that have been employed by the people for over 50,000 years.

> The collection of 13 paintings and 13 photographs tells the traditional stories of the Kunwinjku clans' ancestors. While many stories relate to the Dreamtime, the time of creation, the exhibition also provides an insight into Indigenous culture and the collective knowledge about the seasonal cycles of West Arnhem Land.

The exhibition was purchased by the department in 1994 from the Hogarth Galleries Aboriginal Art Centre, Sydney, and continues to enjoy a successful international touring program. Altogether, the exhibition travelled to many cities around the world, including Bangkok, Shanghai, Singapore, Tokyo, Seoul, Dhaka, Karachi, Mexico City, Manila, Buenos Aires, Caracas, Maracaibo, Bogota, Wellington, Harare, Nairobi, Port Louis, Pretoria, Lagos, Rome, Ottawa, and Port Moresby.[13]

Some Burmese said this was the first time they had ever seen Aboriginal art. It was not possible to verify whether other Aboriginal art exhibitions were ever held in Myanmar; they possibly were, but many years earlier, and few if any Burmese recalled them. In any event, to stage such an exhibition in a country interested in art, and with a very diverse culture, was both appropriate and worthwhile. The Myanmar Government's censors said they had to inspect the paintings to confirm that they were suitable for public exhibition, as they did for all public showings. I doubt that I mentioned this to Canberra, since there had been no serious suggestion that the Myanmar authorities would object to the exhibition (and, in any event, the Deputy Minister for Culture had already agreed to open the exhibition).

---

13   See the media release on the DFAT website at dfat.gov.au/news/media-releases/Pages/seasons-of-the-kunwinjku-aboriginal-art-from-west-arnhem-land.aspx.

Splendours of Arakan book launch, 2001

One of the embassy's modest public diplomacy initiatives during this period was to organise a book launch for Dr Pamela Gutman of Sydney University, whose *Burma's Lost Kingdoms: Splendours of Arakan* was published by Orchid Press, Bangkok, in 2001.[14] Pamela had been my contemporary at ANU in the mid-1960s, and gone on to become one of the world's foremost experts on the middle period of Burmese history. A frequent visitor to Burma during the previous 20 years, Dr Gutman was present at the launch at the ambassador's residence, and was grateful for a chance to acknowledge the superb publication in the company of her many Burmese friends and colleagues who had assisted her in what was her life's work. Not least of these was her photographer friend Zaw Min Yu, a Yangon resident whose unique images grace the book. We were able to assemble a number of Dr Gutman's Burmese academic friends and collaborators at the launch. Being held at the ambassador's residence, the launch was a private event for which regime approval was neither needed nor sought.

Burma–Thailand Railway photographic exhibition, 2003

Another locally inspired event was the exhibition of photos of the Burma–Thailand Railway from the Department of Veterans' Affairs. The photographs were merely exhibition-size copies of black-and-white photographs in the Australian War Memorial's collection, reproduced in larger format and framed simply after their arrival in Yangon. The photographs were later donated to the small 'Death Railway Museum' in Thanbyuzayat, which until then had photographs mainly from Japanese sources. The Department of Veterans' Affairs had also published a memorial monograph to mark the 60th anniversary, *Australians on the Burma–Thailand Railway 1942–43*.[15] The embassy arranged to obtain bulk copies of this publication from

---

14   Pamela Gutman, *Burma's Lost Kingdoms: Splendours of Arakan,* Bangkok: Orchid Press, 2001. For tributes about the book, see books.google.com.au/books/about/Burma_s_lost_kingdoms.html?id=YXJuAAAAMAAJ&redir_esc=y. Pamela Gutman died in Sydney in early 2015. The author's obituary for her was carried by the ANU blog site, *New Mandala*: asiapacific.anu.edu.au/newmandala/?s=Gutman.

15   John Moreman, *Australians on the Burma-Thailand Railway 1942–43*, Canberra: Department of Veterans' Affairs, 2003.

the Department of Veterans' Affairs to have on hand at the exhibition, and the Myanmar Government had no objections to these being distributed. The exhibition was staged at the Yangon Inya Lake Hotel, whose manager at the time was personally interested in the story of the railway. It was significant that the Australian Embassy was able to sell copies of the Australian official account of the railway at this exhibition, since few Burmese knew much about Burma's involvement in World War II, which has long been suppressed by post-independence nationalistic and anti-colonial Burmese governments. There was no attempt whatsoever by the censorship authorities to censor the publication, or to obstruct its dissemination, since it obviously had no political relevance for contemporary Myanmar.

To stage any public event in Myanmar at this time, it was necessary to obtain the permission of the censorship authorities in the Ministry of Home Affairs. There was no evidence of any previous public exhibition of material about the foreign prisoners of war on the Burma–Thailand Railway being held in Myanmar since World War II. So it was by no means certain that permission would be forthcoming, especially given the distorted anti-British view of World War II promoted in the Defence Ministry's own museum. But, thankfully — and perhaps as a sign of things to come much later — in the end, in granting its permission, the ministry merely asked for all references to 'Burma' in captions for photographs to be changed to 'Myanmar/Burma', which in the circumstances was quite a reasonable request. So while this exhibition was very modest in scale and content, it was nevertheless the first public showing in Myanmar of any material about the role that foreign prisoners of war had played in the construction of this railway inside Burma, which tended to be one part of World War II history that the military regime normally preferred not to acknowledge publicly. In other words, this was another sign of opening up and 'normalisation'.

Under the Thein Sein reforms after 2011, permission to open the old railway route to visitors was granted, and Professor Joan Beaumont, an ANU scholar who had worked on museums on the Thai side of the railway, was given permission to visit Three Pagodas Pass in January 2013. I learnt subsequently that plans are under discussion to reopen a new museum about the railway in Thanbyuzayat, possibly as a Mon State project. Arguably, there is a consistent pattern of official interest in the history of the railway, although it has certainly not always enjoyed high priority in Yangon. Some aspects of the way tourism has developed around the railway in Thailand may not be so appealing to more conservative Myanmar taste, but it would not be surprising if this whole area became much more a destination for local as well as overseas visitors. Australian (and British) travel companies specialising in war commemorations had for many years been organising small groups to visit Thanbyuzayat without problems, but they were never allowed to revisit the railway track beyond Wegale, which is only a few kilometres from Thanbuyzayat.

Opera in the Strand Hotel, 2001

A more traditional event organised entirely by the embassy was a recital by Australian soprano Joanna Cole, who approached the embassy in 2001 about the possibility of giving a concert in Yangon. Ms Cole was planning to be travelling in Southeast Asia, and she was interested in visiting Myanmar. As she was paying for her own travel, the costs for the embassy of arranging a recital for her were minimal, so we readily agreed, even though at that stage we had never heard of her.[16] Other Western embassies in Yangon occasionally staged concerts as part of their public diplomacy efforts, so a recital of operatic arias was not impossible to imagine; it had just never been done before, or at least in recent times. The Australian Embassy had never attempted such an ambitious public event in Yangon, and there were no counterpart Burmese classical music organisations — no orchestra, no opera troupe — as Burmese performing arts focused entirely on Burmese classical genres. Neither the Australian nor Myanmar governments had any objections to the idea of the concert.

The recital was staged on 8 October 2001 as a free concert in the prestigious Strand Hotel, located, as it happens, next door to the embassy, and which was at that point celebrating its centenary. Joanna Cole chose her own program, which included arias sung in other settings by none other than Joan Sutherland. The embassy did not presume to pass judgment on the suitability of items for the recital, nor did the Myanmar Government. We tried to invite as many local artists as we could find, but they were not numerous, as Western

---

16   See her CV at wp.morethanopera.com/artists/.

classical music, and opera in particular, had not been much encouraged under the cultural chauvinism of Ne Win's time. The *Myanmar Times* generously provided prominent coverage of the occasion.[17]

---

17 'Diva Hits a High Note for Double Centenary', *Myanmar Times,* 15–21 October 2001, Vol. 5, No. 85.

11

Reflections on Coming to Terms with Myanmar: Personally and as Convener, ANU Burma/Myanmar Update 2004–13

Yangon is a cosmopolitan and multicultural city that was to affect me greatly, both personally at the time and 'professionally' for the next decade after my retirement as an Australian civil servant/diplomat. None of this was predicted by me at the time, nor was it planned. I had greatly enjoyed my unexpected assignment as Australian Ambassador to Myanmar, and indeed had been disappointed when my request for an additional year in the position was not accepted. When I left Myanmar, this could have easily been the end of any interaction I had with Myanmar. That would have ultimately been a great let down, and I would have missed out on ongoing and new experiences in engaging with Myanmar, its people, and occasionally its leaders. Some of my Australian associates on Myanmar may not have even perceived much change in my role after my 'retirement' as a diplomat, but it could have easily been the case of a one-off assignment for me ending after just three years. Although I had no retirement plan on leaving Yangon, I am very glad Myanmar was not a one-off assignment for me.

After I took early retirement from the Department of Foreign Affairs and Trade in August 2003, I was invited to take up a (unpaid) position as Visiting Fellow on Myanmar/Burma in the Department of Political and Social Change, without any specific obligations or work project in mind. So the challenge of 'coming to terms' with Myanmar remained, and for me a number of areas of 'unmet demand' proved to exist in relation to Myanmar, including the need to explain public developments on the basis of some direct experience and knowledge of dealing with leading figures in Myanmar; the need to assess the ongoing discourse about the encouragement or denial of democracy in Myanmar as objectively as possible and to balance the views and counter-views of those involved in the debate; and the need to articulate how and why any particular policy response by the Australian Government would be appropriate or inappropriate. Of course, a number of Australians were quite well qualified to do this, but I was the only former serving Australian diplomat who was absolutely free to comment.[1] Some Australian scholars of Myanmar — such as Monique Skidmore in Canberra and Sean Turnell in Sydney — were frequent commentators for the international media and parliaments, but being in the middle of their careers, they occasionally felt constrained from saying too much. Nicholas Farrelly later joined this 'group' after his return to ANU from Oxford University.[2]

Interestingly, none of us working on Myanmar at ANU ever felt the need to coordinate or consult with each other about what we were saying publicly about Myanmar; we always felt we could do no more than offer our best impartial analysis and assessment. I never experienced any discomfort from comments about Myanmar expressed by these true experts, who became my friends, and I only hope they felt the same. Our views were certainly not identical, and that was never what we sought to achieve, but we all made quite a contribution to understanding Myanmar, not only within Australia but well beyond our shores as well. This was mostly on the basis of being asked to respond instantly about developments that might (or might not) have already been reported with a particular interpretation by members of the Burmese democracy movement. In my case, it certainly helped greatly to have the status of Visiting Fellow at ANU.[3] ANU encouraged its affiliated personnel to speak to the media, without any thought

---

1   For example, my predecessor as ambassador, Lyndall MacLean, was still working as a member of the Department of Foreign Affairs and Trade.

2   He also kindly gave me strong support for this memoir project.

3   In early 2004, I was asked to act as co-convener for ANU Burma Update, and was convener for the six update conferences between 2004 and 2013. The name of the conference was changed: initially to 'Burma/Myanmar Update', and then to 'Myanmar/Burma Update', which was soon shortened to 'Myanmar Update'.

to restricting or controlling what they said, seeing value in their publicising their ANU status. (This eventually became the butt of local comedians' jokes about the ABC and the SBS — the media outlets most frequently using university academics as a free source of 'expert' opinion for their current affairs programs.)

The Australian National University as a Myanmar 'think tank'

In parallel with this, along with the rest of the outside world, the Australian Government had found one way it could try to come to terms with what was happening, and what was not happening, in Myanmar. This was the initiative from around 2000 to financially support The Australian National University's efforts to better understand the various developments and underlying forces at play in Myanmar, and the scope these offered for opening up and encouraging social, political, and economic change: the regular Burma/Myanmar Update Conference. In the decade after 2003, I was to become closely associated with this conference as a co-convener, and edited or co-edited six collections of conference papers.

The conferences, and the publications they spawned, point to the many concerns and problems they uncovered and assessed. I had been invited to give a presentation at the March 2002 conference (while I was still Australian Ambassador and was therefore constrained in what I could say) just 14 months before the 30 May 2003 attack on Aung San Suu Kyi at Depayin. A driving force behind the conferences was Dr Ron May, Associate Professor in the Department of Political and Social Change, who was not a Burma expert but rather a conflict resolution specialist.[4] The format and focus of the update conferences was fairly consistent through this period: it sought to bring the world's leading Burma scholars to Canberra and have them present their interpretations of current events in Myanmar, alongside Burmese scholars and experts. In all cases, the objective was to hear from scholars who had recently been in Myanmar, and were not just examining theoretical or historical

---

4   Under his tutelage, ANU was at the time sponsoring a project on 'Regime Change and Regime Maintenance in Asia and the Pacific', which published a series of research papers.

perspectives. Essentially, the conferences were not political and were not politicised; they endeavoured to consider policy options. The early conferences naturally focused on the debate between 'sanctions versus engagement'.

The themes of the update conferences, and thus the titles and dates of the publications with which I was associated, were:

- *The Illusion of Progress: The Political Economy of Reform in Burma/Myanmar* (2004)
- *Burma's Long Road to National Reconciliation* (2006)
- *The State, Community and the Environment in Myanmar* (2007)
- *Dictatorship, Disorder and Decline in Myanmar* (2008)
- *Ruling Myanmar From Cyclone Nargis to National Elections* (2010)
- *Myanmar's Transition: Openings, Obstacles and Opportunities* (2012)
- *Debating Democratisation in Myanmar* (2014)

An update conference was held in 2003, devoted solely to economic issues and convened by a former ANU colleague, Professor Peter Warr, who has a long-standing and deep interest in and knowledge of Myanmar. No publication was produced from this conference.

Some comments from conveners and editors might be noteworthy. Launching the conference series in 1999/2000, Morten Pedersen, Emily Rudland, and Ron May argued that the military regime was in a strong position rather than a weak one, that 'there are obstacles to the achievement of peace and prosperity in Burma which go beyond the formed structures of government', and that 'the future development of a well-functioning democracy in Burma critically depends on the emergence of a new synergy between a vibrant civil society and a strong, but responsive state'.[5] The argument was not that democracy would be doomed, but 'that it is not inevitable for the armed forces to fall out of power', which 'does not mean giving up hope for a positive political change'.[6]

---

5   See 'Introduction' to Morten B., Pedersen, Emily Rudland and R. J. May (eds), *Burma Myanmar: Strong Regime Weak State*, Adelaide: Crawford House Publishing, 2000, pp. 2–3.
6   Ibid., p. 21.

Papers from the second update conference were not published until after the shock of the 30 May 2003 Depayin incident. Co-conveners David Mathieson and Ron May concluded that 'as promising as many of the events of 2002 were in Burma, progress was largely illusory', and that 'the possible gains [for the regime] from destroying the domestic opposition outweighed any threat from international sanctions'.[7] Many of the conferences' forecasts were nevertheless very prescient. Editing the 2006 publication, I commented that 'national reconciliation is likely to be a drawn-out gradual process rather than a single event or agreement'.[8]

As late as the 2006 and 2008 update conferences, most speakers from Myanmar were anxious about publishing anything abroad that could be viewed by the Myanmar authorities as hostile to the military regime. Even if we treated such speakers as 'commentators' without formal papers, they would not necessarily be exempt from close scrutiny and possible official reprisals. By the time of the 2010 conference, this was no longer a concern, and Myanmar contributors began providing quite frank and revealing chapters. On the whole, Myanmar presenters were chosen for their independence, rather than their political affiliation. Some of our conference presenters from Myanmar — selected also for their ability to influence policy — went on to become advisors to President Thein Sein. It was always hoped that the conference publications would achieve some circulation and sales inside Myanmar, and, largely thanks to the Myanmar Book Company, this happened. By 2013, after reforms were becoming more embedded, copies of *Myanmar's Transition* (2012) were observed in up-country bookshops. Copies of all update conference publications were presented to Aung San Suu Kyi and to the Myanmar Government (even *Dictatorship, Disorder and Decline in Myanmar*, with its cover photo of the 'Saffron Revolution' street protests).

The Myanmar Embassy in Canberra was not formally invited to attend the conferences, although as a courtesy they were always informed beforehand of the program and the speakers. In the early days, their presence at the conference would not have been welcomed by some

---

7   See 'Introduction' and 'A Black Day in Burma/Myanmar' in David S. Mathieson and R. J. May (eds), *The Illusion of Progress: The Political Economy of Reform in Burma/Myanmar*, Adelaide: Crawford House Publishing, 2004, pp. 14, 303.
8   See 'Introduction' to Trevor Wilson (ed.), *Myanmar's Long Road to National Reconciliation*, Singapore: ISEAS Publications, 2006, p. xxxiii.

members of the Burmese expatriate community, regardless of any political associations. In those days, the Myanmar Embassy received reports of the conference from their own supporters who had attended. The embassy did not attend until the 2010 conference, which included a former senior Myanmar diplomat among the speakers. Accordingly, at the 2010 conference, the Myanmar Ambassador (who was known as a supporter of reforms) attended unobtrusively, without notice, and without fuss. No Myanmar Government speaker was invited to the conference until the 2013 conference, when the Deputy Minister for National Planning and Economic Development (a former academic economist) attended. Maintaining a careful distance from politics and from both governments undoubtedly helped the conference. It goes without saying that neither DFAT nor AusAID ever attempted to interfere with the content or character of the conference. In its format, the conference resembled most of the other country update conferences sponsored by ANU.

The Australian National University Myanmar/Burma Update Conference has been unique: nowhere else was there a conference that looked at contemporary Myanmar in a dispassionate way. To a considerable extent, this goal was greatly assisted by the many prominent and respected Burmese who came from Myanmar to speak about how things really were inside Myanmar. Some of them did this at some personal risk. Some prominent international observers of Burma regarded it as a very valuable and significant institution. It achieved considerable profile around the world, among scholars and governments alike. Burma scholars from around the world were prepared to participate in the conferences. Generating specific policy or other outcomes was not the objective of these conferences, but they certainly encouraged networking across borders, and they certainly enhanced Australian understanding of Myanmar. One notable feature was the enduring support and loyalty to the conference shown by Australian NGOs and individuals working with Myanmar, as well as the Australian Government's former aid agency, AusAID.[9]

---

9   On 18 September 2013, the new Australian Prime Minister, Mr Tony Abbott, announced that the Australian Agency for International Development would be integrated into to Department of Foreign Affairs and Trade. Mr Abbott said: 'I intend to recommend to the Governor-General that the Australian Agency for International Development be integrated into the Department of Foreign Affairs and Trade, enabling the aid and diplomatic arms of Australia's international policy agenda to be more closely aligned.' The new Minister for Foreign Affairs, Ms Julie Bishop, was also appointed Minister for International Development.

Epilogue

The glimmers of hope that prompted many to anticipate that change might be coming in Myanmar in 2000 were extinguished in 2003–04 by the actions of the military regime. However, the desire for change and a better life did not disappear. It took a few years for the tide to turn in favour of change, but turn it did: further triggers for significant change could be observed in 2007 (the 'Saffron Revolution'), in 2008 (Cyclone Nargis), and in 2010 (general elections). Myanmar now seems to be one of the few countries undergoing a political transition that is largely, but not entirely, peaceful and which has been sustained for more than a short time. The origins of the changes are largely home-grown and can be traced back to the period around 2000, if not before then. But, unlike some countries, change in Myanmar has been greatly influenced by international factors — much more than the Myanmar military leadership would like to acknowledge, and perhaps somewhat less than many in the international community would recognise or believe should occur.

Yet, realistically and objectively — despite the various stratagems deployed by interested parties from time to time, and despite many outspoken statements and allegations by different parties along the way — Myanmar's problems have been quite steadily set on a 'long road to reconciliation' which will hopefully incorporate reforms more along the lines of what all stakeholders would prefer, or at least could live with, in a more or less ongoing trajectory — one satisfactorily 'owned' by the Myanmar people themselves. Some found it distasteful that, in the case of Myanmar, this 'road' was determined by the military regime; but, pragmatically, without military backing of some kind, the only way to move forward would have probably been through outright conflict. It seemed contrarian in the least, and to some people quite unprincipled, to try to argue that the cause of the democracy movement should not be accepted uncritically or *in toto* as the appropriate way forward, which explains why debates about 'sanctions versus engagement' were conducted so vehemently. Yet surely, if the authoritarian regime is even slightly open to outside ideas and to outside influence, and if it can be demonstrated that communication with — and pressure on — the authoritarian regime has provided concrete examples of compromise and reconciliation, it would be not only foolish but dangerous to ignore what might be called a 'managed approach' to change and transformation.

My overwhelming reaction on observing conditions on the ground was that things were not nearly as bad in Myanmar as they were being presented internationally by the activist movement and the media. Although my opinion was never sought on whether or not 'extra-judicial killings' were widespread and whether or not massive repression of free speech was endemic, I knew that while many people in Myanmar were quite unhappy, many were also managing well enough, and the Myanmar situation did not seem nearly as bad as that in many other countries. Obviously, the wider lessons for effective resolution of deeply intransigent conflict are plainly present in the case of Myanmar — and are probably applicable for other situations. They include the overriding importance of the maximum possible transparency, as a means of reassuring all concerned about the process of change; and, conversely, the risks of unnecessary secrecy, especially because it subverts the benefits of openness; the value of occasional self-restraint in terms of not insisting on one's own interests all the time, when differing interests have to be accommodated at some point; the essentiality of maintaining lines of communication, even when worst-case scenarios ensure; and, ultimately, the folly of a non-inclusive approach that does not involve all possible stakeholders at all times, even those not initially fully committed to a shared outcome.

While The Australian National University awarding an Honorary Doctorate of Letters to Aung San Suu Kyi in 2013 was obviously a high point in any terms, it has been especially gratifying to see and work with some of the students who have won Australian Government scholarships to study for postgraduate degrees after 2010. Their personal and intellectual qualities, as well as their determination to enhance their capabilities to contribute more effectively to Myanmar's development, have been truly exceptional.

The Australian National University decision in 2015 to establish a Myanmar Research Centre in the College of Asia and the Pacific at ANU was also a most appropriate follow-up to this substantial collective effort.

Bibliography

Amnesty International, 'Media Report on First Visit to Myanmar', *World Institute for Asian Studies,* Vol. 12 No. 876. Available at: www.asiantribune.com/news/2003/02/10/amnesty-international-its-first-myanmar-visit.

Aung San Suu Kyi, *Freedom From Fear and Other Writings*, London: Penguin, 1995.

Badgley, John H., Robert H. Taylor, David I. Steinberg, Helen James, Seng Raw, Kyaw Yin Hlaing and Morten B. Pedersen, *Reconciling Burma/Myanmar: Essays on U.S. Relations with Burma*, NBR Analysis, National Bureau of Asian Research, April 2004.

Baker, Mark, 'Suu Kyi Talks on the Way, Downer Told', *The Age*, 3 October 2002. Available at: www.theage.com.au/articles/2002/10/02/1033538672884.html.

Baker, Mark, 'Downer Faces Burma's Tyrants', *The Age*, 5 October 2002. Available at: www.theage.com.au/articles/2002/10/04/1033538774051.html.

Baker, Mark, 'Suu Kyi Attacks Canberra', *The Age*, 7 October 2002.

Beaton, Terry, 'Burma Remembered: An Incredible Experience', *Barbed Wire and Bamboo*, July/August 2003.

Billington, Mike, and Gail Billington, 'US, Not Myanmar is Isolating Itself', *Economist Intelligence Report,* 30 July 2004.

Blaxland, John, 'Myanmar: Time for Australian Defence Cooperation', *Security Challenges,* Vol. 7 No. 4, Summer 2011, pp. 63–76. Available at: www.regionalsecurity.org.au/Resources/Files/vol7no4 Blaxland.pdf.

Buncombe, Andrew, 'Boycott Burma: To go or not to go?', *Independent*, 2 June 2008. Available at: www.independent.co.uk/travel/news-and-advice/boycott-burma-to-go-or-not-to-go-837207.html.

Callahan, Mary, *Making Enemies: War and State Building in Burma*, Singapore: Singapore University Press, 2004.

Clapp, Priscilla, 'Burma's Long Road to Democracy', US Institute for Peace Special Report, New York, November 2007.

Downer, Alexander, 'A Start to Help Set Burmese on the Road to Human Rights', *International Herald Tribune*, 24 August 1999.

Downer, Alexander, 'Burma's Agent of Change', *The Advertiser*, 1 April 2012. Available at: www.adelaidenow.com.au/archive/news/downer-burmas-agent-of-change/story-e6freacl-1226315903405.

Downer, Alexander, 'Burma Visit', Media Release, 3 October 2002. Available at: foreignminister.gov.au/releases/2002/fa144_02.html.

Fukui, Ryu, 'Myanmar de Mieta Chiteki Enjo no Igi to Kadai' ['The Significance of and Issues Experienced in Intellectual Assistance in Myanmar'], *Kokusai Kaihatsu Janaru* [*International Development Journal*], July 2003.

Ganesan, N., 'Myanmar's Foreign Relations: Reaching Out to World', in Kyaw Yin Hlaing, Robert H. Taylor and Tin Maung Maung Than (eds), *Myanmar: Beyond Politics to Societal Imperatives*, Singapore: Institute of Southeast Asian Studies, 2005.

Gifford, Peter, 'The Cold War Across Asia', in Goldsworthy, David (ed.), *Facing North: A Century of Australian Engagement with Asia*, Melbourne: Melbourne University Press, 2001.

Gorman, Michelle, 'Travelling a Track of Sad Memories', *Myanmar Times*, 24 December 2001–6 January 2002, Vol. 5, No. 95–96.

Gutman, Pamela, *Burma's Lost Kingdoms Splendours of Arakan*, Bangkok: Orchid Press, 2001.

Gyngell, Allan, and Michael Wesley, *Making Australian Foreign Policy*, Cambridge: Cambridge University Press, 2003.

Holliday, Ian, 'Rethinking the United States's Myanmar Policy', *Asian Survey*, Vol. 45, No. 4, July/August 2005, pp. 603–621.

Horsey, Richard, *Ending Forced Labour in Myanmar: Engaging a Pariah Regime,* London: Routledge, 2011.

International Crisis Group, 'Burma/Myanmar: How Strong Is the Military Regime?', Asia Report No. 11, Bangkok and Brussels, 21 December 2000.

International Crisis Group, 'Myanmar: The Role of Civil Society', Asia Report No. 27, Bangkok and Brussels, December 2001.

International Labour Office, 'Developments Concerning the Question of the Observance by the Government of Myanmar of the Forced Labour Convention: Report of High Level Team', Geneva, November 2001. Available at: www.ilo.org/public/english/standards/relm/gb/docs/gb282/pdf/gb-4-ax.pdf.

James, Helen, *Security and Sustainable Development in Myanmar,* London: Routledge, 2006.

Kinley, David, and Trevor Wilson, 'Engaging a Pariah: Human Rights Training in Burma/Myanmar', *Human Rights Quarterly,* Vol. 29, No. 2, 2007, pp. 368–402.

Lang, Hazel J., 'The Courage of Aung San Suu Kyi', *Overland,* Issue 183, Winter 2006.

Lintner, Bertil, *Outrage: Burma's Struggle for Democracy,* London and Bangkok: White Lotus, 1990.

Lintner, Bertil, *Aung San Suu Kyi and Burma's Struggle for Democracy,* Bangkok: Silkworm Books, 2011.

Lloyd, Peter, 'Alexander Downer gains little from Burmese meeting', *The World Today,* 3 October 2002. Available at: www.abc.net.au/worldtoday/stories/s692508.htm.

Lowe, David, and Daniel Oakman (eds), *Australia and the Colombo Plan 1949–1957,* Canberra: Australian Government Department of Foreign Affairs and Trade, 2004.

Magnusson, Anna, and Morten Pedersen, *A Good Office?: Twenty Years of UN Mediation in Myanmar,* New York: International Peace Institute, 2012.

Maldon, Chris, 'Newspaper Boss Ross Dunkley to Renew Push for Free Media in Burma', *The Australian*, 2 July 2011. Available at: www.theaustralian.com.au/news/world/newspaper-boss-ross-dunkley-to-renew-push-for-free-media-in-burma/story-e6frg6so-1226085874701.

Mathieson, David S., and R. J. May (eds), *The Illusion of Progress: The Political Economy of Reform in Burma/Myanmar,* Adelaide: Crawford House Publishing, 2004, pp. 14, 303.

Maung Maung, U, *The 1988 Uprising in Burma*. New Haven, Connecticut: Yale University Southeast Asia Studies, 1999.

Mawdsley, James, *The Iron Road: A Stand for Truth and Democracy in Burma,* New York: North Point Press, 2001.

Mitton, Roger, 'Inside "Secret" Meetings: The Chilston Conferences to Engage Yangon', *Asia Week Online*, March 2000.

Moreman, John, *Australians on the Burma–Thailand Railway 1942–43*, Canberra: Department of Veterans' Affairs, 2003.

Morris, Heather, and D. F. Waterhouse, *The Distribution and Importance of Arthropod Pests and Weeds of Agriculture in Myanmar*, Canberra: ACIAR. Available at: aciar.gov.au/files/node/2145/the_distribution_and_importance_of_arthropod_pests_48147.pdf.

Myanmar Times, 'Diva Hits a High Note for Double Centenary', *Myanmar Times,* 15–21 October 2001, Vol. 5, No. 85.

New Light of Myanmar, 'Yangon Landing for Air Race', *New Light of Myanmar,* 13 November 2000.

New Light of Myanmar, 'Aircraft in Sydney Air Race 2001 Stop Over at Yangon International Airport', *New Light of Myanmar*, 27 March 2001.

Pedersen, Morten B., *Promoting Human Rights in Burma: A Critique of Western Sanctions Policies,* Lanham, Maryland: Rowman & Littlefield, 2008.

Pedersen, Morten B., Emily Rudland and R. J. May (eds), *Burma Myanmar: Strong Regime Weak State,* Adelaide: Crawford House Publishing, 2000.

Pedersen, Morten B., and David Kinley (eds), *Principled Engagement: Negotiating Human Rights in Repressive States,* London: Ashgate, 2013.

Popham, Peter, *The Lady and the Peacock: The Life of Aung San Suu Kyi,* New York: The Experiment Publishing, 2012.

Razali Ismail, 'Meetings with Aung San Suu Kyi', *The Irrawaddy,* Vol. 15, No. 4, April 2007.

Richards, Rowley, *A Doctor's War,* Sydney: Harper-Collins, 2005.

Riley, Mark S., and Ravi A. Balaram, 'The United States International Military Education and Training (IMET) Program with Burma/Myanmar: A Review of the 1980–1988 Programming and Prospects for the Future', *Asian Affairs: An American Review,* Vol. 40, No. 3, pp. 109–132.

Saffin, Janelle, 'Burma Emerges from a Shadowy Past, but Real Progress Lies Ahead', *The Conversation,* July 2014.

Selth, Andrew, *Burma's Armed Forces: Power Without Glory,* Norwalk, Connecticut: Eastbridge, 2002.

Skehan, Craig, 'Australian Rights Lawyers Under Fire on Burma', *The Age,* 6 September 2000.

Skehan, Craig, 'Suu Kyi Warming to Rights Seminars', *Sydney Morning Herald,* 20 February 2001.

Skidmore, Monique, *Karaoke Fascism: Burma and the Politics of Fear,* Philadelphia: University of Pennsylvania Press, 2004.

Steinberg, David I., *Burma: The State of Myanmar,* Washington DC: Georgetown University Press, 2001.

Steinberg, David I., 'The United States and Its Allies: The Problem of Burma/Myanmar Policy', *Contemporary Southeast Asia,* Vol. 29, No. 2, August 2007, pp. 219–237.

Steinberg, David I., *Turmoil in Burma: Contested Legitimacies in Myanmar*, Norwalk, Connecticut: EastBridge, 2006.

Tamayama, Kazuo, *Railwaymen in the War: Tales by Japanese Railway Soldiers in Burma*, London: Palgrave Macmillan, 2005.

Turnell, Sean, *Fiery Dragons: Banks, Moneylenders and Microfinance in Burma,* Copenhagen: NIAS Press, 2009.

Wilson, Trevor, 'An Australian Perspective on a Transitional Period in Myanmar: May 2000–May 2003', in David S. Mathieson and R. J. May (eds.), *The Illusion of Progress: The Political Economy of Reform in Burma/Myanmar,* Adelaide: Crawford House Publishing, 2004.

Wilson, Trevor (ed.), *Myanmar's Long Road to National Reconciliation*, Singapore: ISEAS Publications, 2006.

Wilson, Trevor, 'The Use of Normative Processes to Achieve Behaviour Change in Myanmar', in Nick Cheesman, Monique Skidmore and Trevor Wilson (eds), *Ruling Myanmar From Cyclone Nargis to National Elections,* Singapore: ISEAS Publications, 2010.

Wintle, Justin, *Perfect Hostage: A Life of Aung San Suu Kyi*, London: Hutchinson, 2007.

Zaw, Aung, 'Aung Thaung: Burma's Untouchable Minister', *The Irrawaddy*, Vol. 15, No. 6, June 2007.

www.ingramcontent.com/pod-product-compliance
Lightning Source LLC
Chambersburg PA
CBHW060322310326

R18053000001B/R180530PG41927CBX00016B/1